CW01301904

Become a Studying and Learning Machine:

Strategies For the Top of the Class, Promotions, and Smashing Your Goals

By Peter Hollins,

Author and Researcher at petehollins.com

Table of Contents

CHAPTER 1: UNDERSTANDING THE STRUCTURE OF LEARNING   7

HOW TO USE SUCCESSIVE RELEARNING	9
THE STIC FRAMEWORK	20
SCAFFOLDING CONTENT	33

CHAPTER 2: KNOW HOW TO READ INTELLIGENTLY   45

DESCARTES'S READING TIPS	45
SMART HIGHLIGHTING STRATEGIES	55
THE REAP METHOD	67

CHAPTER 3: SHARPENING YOUR MEMORY   77

THE BLURTING METHOD	78
THE POWER OF MEMORY ANCHORS	88

CHAPTER 4: BE STRATEGIC; STAY ORGANIZED 103

THE ZETTELKASTEN METHOD	104
CREATE A SKILL TREE	118
CONCRETENESS FADING	129

CHAPTER 5: MASTERING MINDSET 146

THINKING MODES: FOCUSED OR DIFFUSE?	147
THE PROCRASTINATION EQUATION	158
PLAY MATTERS!	171

Chapter 1: Understanding the Structure of Learning

Imagine the following scenario: You're a law student and there's an important test coming up at the end of the month. You painstakingly work your way through all the material, spending time on each textbook chapter and article, and then the day before the test, you quickly "revise" everything you've learned—i.e., you read through it all again once. On the day of the test, you draw a blank. You can answer a few questions, but you're having a hard time recalling the things you need to. You don't get it; haven't you spent hours and hours "studying"? Haven't you made countless notes? How could it be that all that work amounted to so little in the end?

This is a book about all the ways our assumptions and misconceptions about learning may be getting in the way of us achieving our learning potential. Without realizing it, most of us have acquired a set of unhelpful beliefs, habits, and attitudes from our time in conventional education, and we reflexively turn to these old ways of doing things any time we need to acquire new skills or knowledge.

In the chapters that follow, we'll be looking more closely at the "normal" way of studying, and instead considering more evidence-based, effective alternatives that will get you real results. We'll begin with an understanding of how learning actually takes place and how to structure our approach to match the way our brain naturally incorporates new material.

We'll explore the power of a consistent reading habit and also *how* to read for maximum benefit, we'll look at intelligent ways to boost your memory (and why the standard tips and tricks don't always work), we'll examine all the ways that staying organized can actually improve the quality of your thought, and we'll be reappraising deeper beliefs around work, rest, play, and creativity, and how you can consciously harness their power.

How to Use Successive Relearning

But first, let's return to the law exam and "going blank" after hours of study. This situation is not uncommon, and the reason it happens is this: Your "studying" was not true, genuine practice. You certainly did spend hours reading and making notes, but what you didn't do is spend time practicing the one skill that would matter—retrieving information. Look back at the story and you'll see that you practiced retrieval (i.e., actively recalling information from memory) just *once* in the whole month, and that was during the exam itself—no wonder you didn't find it so easy!

The truth is that effective learning is not automatic. What's more, just because you spend time and effort, it does not mean you are learning. **Learning is only effective if it is strategic and actually reflects and supports the way your brain genuinely acquires new skills and knowledge**. That means that if we truly want to learn, we need a deliberate and proven approach, rather than merely defaulting to habitual study techniques that seem like a good idea—reading, highlighting text, making notes.

Knowing how to learn is itself a skill, and it's the reason you're reading this book right now. To learn well, we need to understand how the human mind works so we can optimize. No matter what topic you're trying to master or your current level of achievement, there is an underlying structure and logic to all learning processes, and if you understand that structure, you can make sure to spend your time and effort in the best possible way.

One key pillar in the structure of learning is called **successive relearning**, which is a meta-strategy that combines two smaller strategies: retrieval practice (or the "testing effect") and spaced practice. This combination has plenty of research supporting its effectiveness, particularly for learning vocabulary and terminology (Bahrick 1979; Rawson & Dunlosky 2011; Rawson et al. 2020). Some studies show that just one good relearning session can measurably improve your ability to recall material (Rawson et al. 2018).

In another study, psychology students scored ten percent higher (that's one whole grade letter) when they used a successive relearning approach compared to students who didn't (Rawson et al. 2013). Even more impressive, when tested a month later, these students showed a *forty percent higher* score than those who just bumbled along with no real strategy—suggesting that effects may compound over time.

So, what exactly is this method? Simply, it involves **repeatedly testing yourself on what you've already learned (retrieval practice) over spaced intervals in time (spaced practice)**. Doesn't sound like much, right? The key, however, is that to learn well, you need to actually practice the skill you're trying to improve. For example, if you want to be better at recalling certain information for a test, then you do so by repeatedly practicing recalling that information in the same way as you would be expected to do during a test. Reading, taking notes, listening to lectures, and highlighting are all useful skills, but practicing them will not make it any easier for you to take that test, which is an entirely different set of skills.

If we return to our example of the law exam, a better way to study might include repeatedly doing past papers or test questions that resemble the ones you're likely to encounter. That way, by the time the test arrives, you've already practiced recalling that information so many times that it's easy to simply do it again. Without successive relearning, however, you're not only asking yourself to recall information for the very first time, but you're trying to do so under stressful and high-stakes test conditions.

Successive relearning, according to learning expert Bill Cerbin, involves just four essential features:

1. **Retrieval Practice**: Self-testing is the primary mode. This means actively *recalling* information rather than simply *reviewing* it passively. This may seem like a small distinction, but it makes all the difference in the world.
2. **Spaced Practice**: Practice sessions are spaced out evenly over time, with several sessions scheduled, each separated by one or more days. This spaced repetition enhances long-term retention because every successive attempt reinforces and solidifies the learning that has already been banked.
3. **Mastery of Content**: You continue practicing until you can answer each question correctly at least once during each practice session. This ensures a thorough understanding and retention of the material, but also gives you a concrete way to monitor and track your progress—you should never be unclear about where you are relative to your ultimate study goals.

4. **Repeated Practice**: All questions are practiced multiple times across the sessions—even if you get questions right. This repetition strengthens memory and reinforces learning. Remember that you are trying to practice the skill you actually want to have. If you want to easily and quickly answer questions correctly, then keep practicing easily and quickly answering questions correctly!

Now, while the above principles may seem straightforward in theory, they do require a mindset shift and a little discipline to consistently apply to your study sessions. The biggest threat to effective learning is not a lack of ability or intelligence—it may actually be *complacency*. If we get complacent, we stop paying close attention to what we're actually doing and fall into mindless rote and habit. We may create for ourselves the illusion that we are learning something, when really, we are just "going through the motions."

Let's consider another example. Say you're studying for an anatomy exam. For those who have ever taken an anatomy class, you'll know that there is a seemingly infinite number of new terms and concepts to memorize. Med students, for example, need to know the Latin name of every bone, muscle, ligament, and tendon. Such a student may have an exam coming up where they will be expected to recall dozens of names for parts of the brain.

An ineffective approach may be to sit down with an anatomy textbook and pore over the labeled diagrams of the brain, reading and re-reading the labels. A slightly better but still ineffective approach may be to master the etymological root of each word and hope that an understanding of the Latin name will help you better recall the structure and location of the brain area in question (for example, you may remember that "occipital" literally means "back of the head" in Latin, so locating it on a diagram is easy).

These approaches won't get you far, though. To use a more effective successive relearning approach, you could instead schedule multiple practice sessions, each spaced one to two days apart. During these sessions, you could *repeatedly test and retest yourself* on all the brain terminology you need to know, until you can correctly label every area on a blank diagram—just as you would be expected to do in an exam situation.

You could divide the brain into four sections, tackling each in succession, then moving on, practicing section one and two together, then later section three and four together. Finally, you could build up to practicing all four sections in one practice session. In each session, you are deliberately giving yourself as many opportunities as possible to actively recall the necessary information. One obvious way to do this is to repeatedly give yourself a blank, unlabeled brain diagram and practice recalling the relevant labels. You don't just do this once or twice at the end of a study session; rather, this repeated practice *is* the study session.

Furthermore, much of your learning will actually take place between practice sessions. For example, you may start every anatomy relearning session exactly the same way—you immediately present yourself with the blank brain diagram and practice labeling it a few times. This forces your brain to recall everything it learned from the previous session. In a way, this between-session recall is more important than the recall you practice during a session.

Of course, the exact way that you apply the successive relearning strategy depends on your study topic, your level of learning, your goals, and your unique preferences and limitations. One thing you may immediately notice is that **successive relearning requires time**. If you wish to use your time wisely, you need to be prepared and organized enough to schedule learning sessions and stick to the schedule you set for yourself.

Here are a few steps to get you started:

I. Choose Your Material: First decide what you need to learn. For example, if you're studying biology, you might focus on cell structure and functions. Where your focus should be may be fairly obvious if you're preparing for an exam, but less obvious if your goal is to more generally master some skill or piece of knowledge. When choosing your materials, try to actively connect your learning to your goals. If you're in school or college, it makes sense to align with the learning outcomes provided externally, but if you're a self-directed learner, you may need to spend a little more time thinking about exactly what it is you wish to achieve. Then choose only the material that leads you directly to that outcome.

II. Create Questions: Create questions or activities that cover everything you need to learn in a systematic way. In our biology example, these questions might reference cell structure and functions, such as "What is the function of the nucleus?" or "What organelle is responsible for energy production?" On a broader level, you also need to have a sense of how questions are organized, since this will help you properly schedule relearning sessions. For example, if you have a biology exam on the cell, you may need to assign a textbook chapter to each relearning session, or perhaps organize your questions and activities according to the structure of your exam (i.e., one session spent on multiple choice questions, one on essay questions, one on short answers, etc.)

III. Schedule Practice Sessions: Plan when you'll practice, bearing in mind that the ideal interval for spaced repetition is usually every other day. So, if your biology exam is in two weeks, schedule practice sessions every two days (you could use the days in between to revise some other subject).

IV. Practice Session I: Start with your pre-scheduled questions and activities. Answer each question and check it against the correct answer. For a simple example, if you answer, "The nucleus controls cell activities," for the question about the nucleus, check if that matches the correct answer. Make notes about the questions that are most challenging or those you get wrong and adjust as you go.

Keep practicing until you can answer every question correctly at least once. Use incorrect answers to identify areas where you need more study, and keep attempting them until you get it right. You can consider yourself done with the session once you've answered all questions correctly. Doing things this way gives you a goal to aim for and keeps you focused, but it also helps with motivation since every correct answer is a mini-reward and positive reinforcement for what is working. Proving to yourself again and again that you can do the task at hand will build confidence and go a long way to reducing pre-test nervousness.

V. Practice Session 2: Repeat the process from the first session, moving through each portion of the work you need to do. Staying disciplined and sticking to the schedule is necessary, but don't feel like you can't make adjustments as you go along. Add any new material covered in class since the last session, and reorganize material if you've under- or overestimated how long you'll need to tackle it.

Keep reminding yourself of the two factors that make this kind of process work: *retrieval* and *spaced practice*. As long as you are giving yourself ample opportunity to recall material, and doing so over regular intervals, you will progress. One final caveat: Be careful not to confuse revising/reading with actual retrieval. For example, simply reading over the functions of the different cell organelles and highlighting your textbook as you go is not retrieval practice; answering questions about those functions without consulting your textbook is.

The STIC Framework

If you master the combination of retrieval practice plus spaced repetition, you will instantly discover that your recall improves and that you feel more confident not just with tests but with the material in general. In this chapter, we'll look at a few more factors that set a truly effective approach apart from a mediocre one. If you've ever completed a study session and had the creeping sensation that you wasted your time, then you will already suspect that not all study hours are created equal.

What really *works* when it comes to studying effectively? There are so, so many perspectives and opinions out there, but there are only a handful of principles supported by rigorous evidence. One such approach is the STIC framework for effective learning, which is actually four different factors—two of which we've already covered.

The STIC acronym stands for four crucial principles that can be applied to any subject or topic you're trying to grasp. These principles are:

(S)pacing

(T)esting

(I)nterleaving

(C)ategorizing

Building these four principles into your study routine can make you much more effective, efficient, and best of all, relaxed. You can learn more in less time, and stress less while doing so.

Testing

Also known as active recall, testing is the most critical factor in enhancing exam performance and results—and that applies even if you're not preparing for a test or will never even do one. A test is not merely an external marker of your success, but evidence of your recall ability.

It's understandable that many students resist testing themselves—through years of school, some of us may have been heavily conditioned to think of tests as seriously unpleasant. We may hold plenty of unconscious beliefs that tests are a necessary evil, or something to fear or interpret as a threat because they say something about our intelligence or value as people.

It's worth pushing past this resistance, however, for two reasons. The first is that we've already seen that there are real benefits to learning in this way, but the second is that

testing yourself actually makes learning a lot easier and clearer in the long run.

You will save time and stress by studying this way, and it quickly becomes automatic once you've gotten used to it. If you find that you dread the idea of testing, try shifting your perspective by re-labeling it as a game or a puzzle. Keep curious and don't be hard on yourself. The more you can accept the process of testing, marking, adjusting, and retesting, the more comfortable you will feel with it.

Testing *before* fully learning a topic primes the brain for better retention, even when mistakes are made, leading to better long-term recall. Testing *after* you've learned cements your knowledge, but also shines a handy spotlight on exactly those areas that still need a little more of your attention.

Spacing

Spaced repetition, as we've already seen, involves spreading out study sessions on the same topic over time. This technique contrasts with another, more popular approach that you might be familiar with: cramming!

Imagine that learning is a little like strengthening a muscle over time. If you wanted to grow muscle strength in the gym, you'd understand that it wasn't possible to simply go to the gym once and train ultra-hard for five hours and then hope that this would bring results. Instead, you'd realize that graining strength was a process requiring time, and you'd opt for shorter, more consistent sessions that you completed again and again and again. After every gym session, your muscles would adapt and grow, and these effects would compound over time. It's the same for learning!

Another way to appreciate the value of spaced repetition is to understand the "forgetting curve." To simplify this concept: Your brain will steadily forget whatever it's learned within around three days. You can picture a graph where your retention steeply drops off from one hundred percent down to almost zero percent over those three days. But, every time you revisit your material, you bounce that curve back up again; by reminding yourself of the material, your retention again rises to one hundred percent.

Psychologist Hermann Ebbinghaus was the first to describe this phenomenon in the nineteenth century, and his work revealed that retained information declines in an exponential fashion. More than half of it is lost within just two days, and by the time three months have passed with no revisiting or repetition, about ninety percent is lost and forgotten. Of course, these figures are just estimates, and the exact curve will vary considerably between individuals and depending on the topic, the level of difficulty, interest levels, and so on. The phenomenon remains robust and predictable, however.

You're probably wondering if this means that you can only hope to remember something if you keep revisiting it every three days for the rest of time. Thankfully, the answer is no, and this is why: Every time you revisit the material, the forgetting curve becomes a little bit less steep.

For example, the second time you revisit the material, it takes you four or five days to gradually forget and reach the lowest levels of retention again. The third time, the forgetting curve flattens even further, and you only forget after eight or nine or ten days. Eventually, the curve becomes so flat that in effect you have permanently retained that material.

The trick is, of course, to get in there with practice and repetition *before* you forget (otherwise you will merely be starting over again). In addition, the more repetitions you make at recalling and revisiting the same information, the sooner you flatten that forgetting curve. This is important: **It's not necessarily the total number of hours you spend learning, or the intensity of that learning session, but rather the *number of times* you revisit it.** That means that even a few minutes of active recall will have a positive effect on your overall retention. It also means that a massive, grueling cram session will only bring the benefits of a single "revisit"!

For instance, if you're teaching yourself a new skill like pottery, dedicate specific time slots throughout the week to practice your skills or work on projects. After each study session, take breaks and allow some time to elapse before revisiting the material in subsequent sessions. This spaced repetition enhances memory consolidation and improves your ability to recall information when needed. Where possible, break your available time down into pieces and distribute these pieces evenly throughout your weekly or monthly schedule.

For example, it will be far more effective (not to mention, easier!) to attempt one hour per day than to cram seven hours into every weekend, even though the total time will be the same.

So much for testing and spacing, but what about the other two factors?

These factors are relatively less impactful than the first two, but they are still important and will help you optimize further.

Categorizing

Categorizing, as the name suggests, involves structuring information into categories or themes. Most of us tend to do a little of this automatically, but it's worth paying close attention to how you organize, rank, and break down the various components of your chosen field of study. The way that you break down concepts has an enormous impact on the way that your brain can then absorb and internalize those concepts. In every case, it will be far **easier to process discrete and manageable chunks of information that logically relate to one another** than it is to wade through chaotic pieces of information that are only vaguely or incorrectly connected.

Research indicates that learners who correctly categorize information outperform those who attempt to memorize it as a whole. Visualizing knowledge as a tree with branches and leaves reflects the brain's natural tendency to compartmentalize information—in other words, this is the way your mind *wants* to absorb new data.

Categorizing proves particularly effective for organizing larger amounts of information, or for topics that are complex. Being organized and systematic is not just a habit to keep you neat and tidy, but a matter of ensuring you're making things as clean and streamlined as possible for your brain to manage.

Being well organized also means you have less to remember. Look at the following two example shopping lists and quickly test yourself right now to see which one is easier to remember:

List 1

Apples

Pears

Oranges

Milk

Cheese

Yogurt

Flowers

Chocolate

Valentine's card

List 2

Salt

Cabbage

Cat food

Chicken nuggets

Pears

Shampoo

Bleach

Burgers

Carrots

You can probably tell that it's far easier to remember three categories, and the three items within each category (the first list), than to remember nine distinct and unrelated items (the second list).

Using categorization condenses information and improves your memory since items are meaningfully connected to one another. In this example, the items are all connected thematically, but they can relate to one another in all different ways—i.e., you can categorize concepts according to some other factor. In our shopping list example, this could mean categorizing according to the ingredients required for a specific dish, food versus non-food items, items required for different family members, or other factors such as urgency, color, size, or cost.

Naturally, your categorizations will be a little more abstract, but the principle stays the same. For example, if you're learning about world history, create a timeline or thematic map that categorizes historical events into different periods or themes. You can use color-coded notes or digital mind mapping tools to visually represent the connections between events, figures, and concepts. Breaking down the material into categories enables you to grasp the overarching themes and concepts more effectively, facilitating deeper understanding and retention. The only rule is that the categorization genuinely makes sense to you and aids, rather than hinders, your understanding.

Interleaving

Interleaving encourages mixing up practice within study sessions, helping you cultivate adaptability. The idea is basically to "mix it up" in a strategic way. Unlike blocked practice, which focuses on singular topics for extended periods, **interleaving involves alternating between different subjects or topics within the same study session**. To extend our gym metaphor from earlier, this is a little like training your upper body for a while, then switching to your lower body, then doing your core before returning to upper body again.

This approach strengthens memory associations over time and encourages varied problem-solving strategies. You make the most effective use of your time by working on one skill while you "rest" another. This increases your cognitive flexibility while making intelligent use of every available spot on your schedule.

Although interleaving may initially feel challenging, it leads to better long-term exam performance by improving memory retention. Additionally, interleaving ensures distributed practice, which prevents you from consecutive repetitions of the same task—actively preventing this complacency means that your learning goes much, much deeper.

For instance, if you're studying multiple subjects independently, alternate between different subjects or topics during your study sessions. Rather than focusing solely on one subject for an extended period, spend shorter intervals on each subject, rotating between them regularly. This approach keeps your brain actively engaged and prevents boredom or burnout from prolonged focus on a single topic. Despite it being a little more effortful to schedule, you may find in time that this lowers the cognitive load and creates a more manageable series of smaller chunks rather than too many larger, overwhelming ones.

There are a few things to bear in mind, however, to make sure that you're gaining the benefits of interleaving without it turning into fractured multitasking:

- Experiment with the length of time you spend on each task. Ideally, you should aim to switch tasks just after your peak cognitive performance feels like it's waning. It's a good idea to "end on a high note" so you have something enjoyable to pick up on the next time you revisit that topic. Less is often more; start with short sessions and adjust accordingly, bearing in mind that different subjects and topics may require different time periods.
- If you like, you can also experiment with varying your study materials and resources. You stay with the same topic and subject, but you switch up the format—for example, you toggle between textbooks, online tutorials, audio recordings, and practice exercises to expose yourself to different perspectives and reinforce learning from different sources. Consider it "cross training" for the brain!

- Pay attention whenever things are starting to feel a bit boring, easy, or predictable. This is a sure sign you need to switch things up and challenge yourself.
- Avoid doing practice questions or activities that all take on the exact same format—for example, attempting twenty long division problems one after the other. This is because you will already know that you need the same strategy each time, and you're not learning how to recognize the long division problem when it appears mixed in with other math problems. Interleaving helps you train your ability to *discern particular types of problems* and learn to switch tactics depending on the challenge at hand.
- If you find interleaving difficult, that's okay—it is, but that's because it's more effective. As long as you are feeling comfortably challenged rather than overwhelmed, confused, or distracted, then rest assured that you are building valuable new skills. While you may feel that this form of learning actually impairs performance in the study session itself, it ultimately boosts your performance later on when it will really matter.

Scaffolding Content

Leo Vygotsky was a Russian psychologist renowned for his theories on education, in particular a conception he called the "zone of proximal development," or ZPD. **The ZPD is simply the difference between a student's "actual developmental level as determined by independent problem-solving" and their "potential development as determined through problem-solving under adult guidance or in collaboration with more capable peers"** (Vygotsky 1978).

Vygotsky's genius was to recognize that innate intelligence was not the most important factor in how a child (or in our case, a student of any age) learned. Rather, Vygotsky theorized that learning was essentially a social experience and resulted from interaction with the environment—particularly with other people who are more capable than oneself.

People do not merely have a fixed ability, say, the ability to ride a bike. Rather, we can imagine that they possess a *range* of abilities. Picture a series of three concentric circles—the smallest inner circle is what can be done alone and unsupported, and the larger circle is what cannot be done at all. In between is a special middle zone—the zone of proximal development—which includes all those things *we can do with help*. The following diagram from Indeed.com shows this clearly:

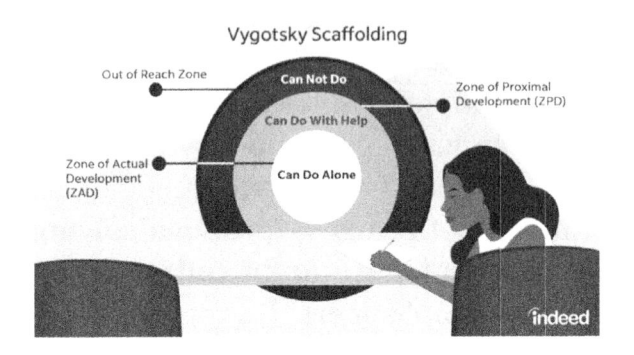

Vygotsky Scaffolding

- Out of Reach Zone
- Can Not Do — Zone of Proximal Development (ZPD)
- Can Do With Help
- Zone of Actual Development (ZAD)
- Can Do Alone

According to Vygotsky, this is the place where learning and development really happen. For example, a child may be able to balance on a stationary bike (actual ability) without being able to properly ride it (actual riding is in the out-of-reach zone). When an adult holds the bike and supports them, however, the child can pedal a little and steer. This sort-of ability falls within the ZPD and is the kind of skill that will eventually allow the child to link their current ability (balancing on a stationary bike) to what they cannot do (riding the bike unaided).

If we are merely operating in the innermost circle, continuing to repeat all the things we already know how to do, we cannot be said to be learning. On the other hand, repeatedly attempting tasks that we simply cannot manage and which are beyond our abilities will also not result in any learning. **Rather, we learn when we are in that Goldilocks zone of proximal development, which acts as a bridge from one to the other.**

This is where the idea of scaffolding comes from—in educational settings, teachers are encouraged to help students learn by giving them structured support that is perfectly calibrated to their unique ZPD. This support lessens as students get better at the subject and become more independent, but to do that effectively, the teacher needs to have a genuine understanding of what that student already knows and what they don't.

In the past, people may have not quite recognized the value of a task done with assistance, thinking that only a task completed independently qualified as real learning. It may be, however, that the ability to bootstrap other people's help is precisely how you learn to do things independently. After all, very few people are going to go directly from not knowing how to do something to immediately knowing how—there's going to be a wobbly intermediate stage, and that's a good thing! In fact, a child with a large ZPD may ultimately achieve more than a child with a small one, even if the first child is by some measures less intelligent or talented. In other words, the ability to gradually move toward mastery with help and guidance is more important than innate, independent ability.

If you're reading this book, chances are you are not in school anymore and the tasks you face are a little more complex than riding a bike. Furthermore, you may be a self-directed learner who is not expected to write exams or follow any particular curriculum, and you may have no formal tutor or teacher to consult for guidance and support. Even still, the same principles apply, and you can use Vygotsky's theory and the scaffolding principle to successfully guide your own learning.

How to Apply Scaffolding to Your Own Learning Process

Assess Your Zone of Proximal Development

Before embarking on any self-learning project, it's crucial to honestly and accurately assess your current understanding of the topic. This step involves reflecting on your existing knowledge and skills related to the subject matter. You can do this by taking self-assessment quizzes, reviewing relevant resources, or analyzing your past experiences.

Try to do this without judgment and go beyond mere ranking and grading, instead becoming curious about exactly what you know, your strengths, and current gaps in your understanding.

For example, if you're learning a new programming language, you might assess your familiarity with basic coding concepts or your experience with languages like Python or Java. What programming tasks can you do with relative ease? Which ones are totally beyond you? At what point exactly do you start finding things tricky? What programming tasks can you currently do so long as you have a little help from someone else or can quickly Google an answer? Those things will most likely be in your ZPD.

Basically, you want to establish the three concentric circles of knowledge for yourself so that you can identify your own ZPD and where it may start and end. Depending on your chosen field of learning, you may find that there is a pre-existing way to grade knowledge—for example, in standardized tests and levels. One example is music grades. If you want to see where your current skill level is when it comes to playing the piano, compare your abilities against learning outcomes for each musical grade and see where you fall.

Set a Goal for Learning

Once you have a clear picture of your unique ZPD, you have a starting point from which you can begin your learning. Knowing the ideal place to start means you don't waste time with material that won't be challenging enough, but you also avoid engaging with work that may be so challenging that it demoralizes you.

Knowing where to start will also help you set a specific learning goal. This goal should be achievable and well-aligned with your aspirations. For instance, if you're learning photography, your goal might be to master the manual settings of your camera within three months, or to produce an image of a standard comparable to that of a certain admired professional. Other goals could include winning a competition, taking part in a performance or recital, creating something, doing work you feel comfortable charging a fee for, publishing or sharing your work, or reaching some other milestone that you've set for yourself.

It's important that this goal is realistic for you and that you can definitely tell when it's been achieved. In other words, "get better" is just too vague and will not inspire or focus you, since how will you ever know what counts as "better"? You may need a hierarchy of successive goals. For example, the main goal is being able to fluently speak Spanish while in Spain, but to reach this you need to achieve several smaller goals, such as working through a series of language books and lectures, mastering certain vocabulary words, watching lectures and Spanish language videos, etc. As you can see, a good goal is one that lays out a clear path of *action*.

Plan Instructional Supports

The strength of using scaffolding and the ZPD theory is that you achieve your goals step by step. Break down your learning goal into smaller, manageable steps or learning objectives. Identify the instructional supports or resources you'll need to achieve each step. For example, if your goal is to improve your public speaking skills, you might plan to watch instructional videos on effective presentation techniques, practice speaking in front of a mirror, and seek feedback from a mentor or peer. If you don't have a wise mentor to guide you, think of ways you can be that person for yourself.

Remember that the ZPD theory tells us that learning is not just a cognitive process—it's a relational and affective (emotional) one. This means that you need to plan steps toward your goal that are not just realistic and practical, but also allow you to stay motivated while challenging yourself. Take the time to stop and acknowledge your progress, reward yourself, and celebrate your achievements. It may help to literally ask yourself what a kind and knowledgeable mentor would say in every situation, and then imagine that their voice is your own internal self-talk.

"Okay, that didn't work . . . but why? Just slow down and take a closer look. You can do this."

"That's great. Now what's the next step?"

"I need to carefully think through this part. Who can I ask for help? Why am I getting this wrong, and what will help me get over this hump?"

"Well done, you did that right!"

Monitor Your Progress

Continually track your advance toward your learning goal. Keep a journal or use a progress-tracking tool to record your achievements, challenges, and areas for improvement. Regularly assess your understanding of the topic, and adjust your learning strategies accordingly—it's difficult to appreciate how far you've really come until you pause and take a look at your progress. The more you can acknowledge and reinforce your achievements, the more motivated you'll be.

Furthermore, monitoring yourself means you quickly spot areas where improvement is necessary—and this empowers you enormously.

Let's say you're learning an instrument, and by monitoring your daily and weekly progress, you notice that you're steadily improving. One day, you feel frustrated with a particular exercise and think, "This is hopeless. I'll never get this right." However, looking back at cold hard data reminds you that you've actually been in this position before and *did* find a way forward. This encourages you to keep going.

Let's also say that on reviewing your records, you notice that you're not putting in as much time doing scales as you originally committed to. You decide that you need to improve on this, but this change would not have been possible unless you were keeping a close eye on how you were using your time over the long term.

Fade Support Over Time

As you gain confidence and proficiency in the topic, gradually reduce your reliance on external support—and it's important that you do it *gradually*! For example, if you've been following online tutorials to learn to use some graphic design software, you might start experimenting with the software on your own without referring to the tutorials as often. Look at the tricks and shortcuts that you currently have in place and find creative ways to progressively do without them.

If you want to be a better cook, gradually rely less and less on recipes and tutorials, and do more on your own. If you're using books, guides, cheat sheets, and other online resources to help you through tricky patches of study, slowly challenge yourself to try to manage without them.

This principle can be combined with the idea of testing from the previous section: Every time you test yourself, you are essentially removing crucial support and checking how well you can fare independently. Practice this by regularly challenging yourself to recall material without referring to a book or double-checking some other resource. By gradually fading support over time, you'll develop greater independence and self-reliance in your self-learning journey.

Summary:

- There are many misconceptions around learning, the primary one is that learning is automatic. Rather, knowing how to learn is itself a skill. Not all learning is created equal, and learning is only effective if it is strategic and reflects and supports the way

your brain naturally acquires new skills and knowledge.
- Successive relearning is a structured approach and consists of a combination of retrieval practice and spaced practice. The process involves repeatedly testing yourself on what you've already learned over spaced intervals in time. Repetition helps; keep practicing until you attain mastery. Don't just review, but recall and track your progress as you go.
- The STIC framework is a proven model encompassing spacing, testing, interleaving, and categorizing. Testing enhances recall; spacing maximizes the number of study "reps" you do and counters the effects of the forgetting curve; it's not necessarily the total number of hours you spend learning, or the intensity of that learning session, but rather the *number of times* you revisit that matters most.
- Categorizing involves structuring information into categories or themes. It's easier to process manageable chunks of information that logically relate meaningfully to one another. This also improves your memory. With interleaving we alternate between different subjects or topics within the same study session.

Distributed practice is difficult but cultivates mental flexibility.
- The zone of proximal development is the space between a student's independent ability and what they can achieve with help and support. To "scaffold" your own learning and build competence step by step, challenge yourself to stay in this zone—i.e., create "mental training wheels." Set manageable goals, calibrate your learning well, and fade support over time, gradually removing scaffolds as you improve.

Chapter 2: Know How to Read Intelligently

There are some disciplines and skills that require very little "book learning," such as dance, athletics, or music. For most of us, however, our chosen topic of study will sooner or later require a little reading—or a lot. Even if our chosen discipline is not book-heavy, we can almost always derive some benefit from reading about it in one way or another. In this chapter we'll be looking at ways to fine tune your reading skills so that you can get the greatest benefits from the best learning tool humankind has ever invented: books.

<u>Descartes's Reading Tips</u>

What is your attitude to reading?

In your world, what is reading really *for*, and what place does it have in your everyday life?

For the world's most learned and accomplished people, the answer to the above is that reading is simply *everything*. There are very few great thinkers, talented masters, or other intellectual heavyweights who don't have reading as a central feature of daily life. **If you want to learn, in other words, you need to know how to read**. Yet so few of us are actively taught how to go about it.

First, reading serves various purposes: entertainment, inspiration, distraction, knowledge acquisition, or a combination of all of these. Not every instance of reading needs to reach PhD levels of profundity or be supremely useful, but if we are thinking about reading to learn, we need to understand how to read in a strategic, deliberate, and focused way.

We can think of reading as far more than mere input; it's an *active* means to expand knowledge, find meaning, understand others and oneself, discover, and improve life while minimizing mistakes. As David Ogilvy aptly put it, "Reading furnishes the mind and enriches life." **Reading is, essentially, an adjunct to and expansion of our own consciousness.**

Farnam Street or FS blog has a great tagline: "Mastering the best that other people have already figured out," and this neatly encapsulates one of reading's key benefits. Through books, we access a wealth of accumulated knowledge often recycled from the past. By drawing on the wealth of knowledge and understanding already laid down in countless written works, we are granted access to more intellectual territory than we could ever secure on our own. (In a way, we drastically expand our zone of proximal development! Think of all the things we could achieve with the help of every great thinker from the whole of history . . .)

Read in any way you can, and that includes borrowing from libraries, reading online pdfs and copies, or accessing eBooks. If possible, however, try to own hard copies of books since this allows a certain familiarity and encourages a deeper grasp of its material, since you can annotate the book exactly as you like and return to its pages again and again.

Take a look at the following advice for how to read a book (in particular, a work of philosophy):

> "I should like the reader first of all to go quickly through the whole book like a novel, without straining his attention too much or stopping at the difficulties which may be encountered. The aim

should be merely to ascertain in a general way the matters I have dealt with. After this, if he finds that these matters deserve to be examined and he has the curiosity to ascertain their causes, he may read the book a second time in order to observe how my arguments follow. But if he is not able to see this fully, or if he does not understand all the arguments, he should not give up at once. He should merely mark with a pen the places where he finds the difficulties and continue to read on to the end without a break. If he then takes up the book for a third time, I venture to think he will find the solutions to most of the difficulties he marked before; and if any still remain, he will discover their solution on a final re-reading."

The passage comes from *The Philosophical Writings of Descartes* by John Cottingham et al. and comes to us from a time when the printing press had only recently been invented—*it was written in 1644.* Advice about how best to read, then, has not changed all that much for almost four hundred years!

When Descartes was writing, the majority of the population was illiterate, and most information came from the learned class or the authority of the Catholic Church. Descartes, however, understood that **knowing how to read was a powerful technology that could allow anyone to discover truth for themselves**—provided they learned how and applied a set of simple rules to aid their comprehension.

Descartes's goal was to "aim over the heads of the academics and reach the man and woman of *bon sens,*" that is, "good sense" and reason. The quote above reflects the four simple rules Descartes reiterated as essential for proper reading:

1. Read through everything quickly to gain a general idea of what the work is about.
2. Read through again, but this time paying attention to the underlying structure of the arguments being put forward. If these are unclear, use a pen to mark the tricky places.
3. Read through a third time, keeping all your problems and questions from step 2 in mind, and try to gain a deeper understanding of how the text fits into the framework of the overall argument.
4. Finally, if you're still confused, reread it yet again.

And there you have it. The secret to reading well, according to Descartes, anyway, is not some gimmicky "speed reading" trick or to cheat with study guides or summaries. Instead, Descartes suggests you read—a lot—and then read some more. A particularly meaty volume may well require four attempts or even more, but with each pass you deepen your understanding.

You might be thinking, "I can't even find time to read a book once, let alone four times!" And this takes us neatly to the next point, which is of course how to find more time to read.

Reading Is a Choice

It bears repeating, but the people who think it excessive to commit an hour a day to reading are also the same people who will easily commit five, six, or seven hours to watching TV, gaming, or mindlessly scrolling social media. The truth is, a solid reading habit takes energy and effort. You need to set a goal and commit to it, and do so **consistently**, even though it would be easier and more enjoyable in many ways to watch TV and so on.

If you find yourself saying, "I don't have enough time" (for reading or indeed any enriching activity), mentally translate what you are really saying: "This is not a priority for me. I want to choose something else." If you are committed to the benefits that reading brings, then there will be enough time because you will *make* time.

If you need convincing, simply observe yourself for a week and track every minute and hour that you spend on pointless or even harmful habits. Then convert this and see what would be possible for you if you dropped this habit and used that time to read instead.

If a person spends three to four hours every day watching TV or messing around on their phones, and perhaps an additional two or three hours commuting or grocery shopping, that's easily twenty-eight hours a week, every week. That's 112 hours a month, and 1344 hours a year—and that may be on the lower end. Let's say you can read a page a minute. With 1344 hours a year, that translates to 80,640 pages of text—and that's *more than two hundred full-sized books per year.*

These figures are not fantastical. That time already exists, right now, in your schedule, but is currently being invested (wasted?) on something else. What might your life look like two hundred books from now?

At this rate, in ten years, that becomes two thousand books. Over a lifetime, who knows how many. Every book is not just an item on a list, but a potential invitation into deeper knowledge, a link to richer ideas, and a chance to create a more sophisticated, more intelligent working model of the world around you. In other words, the value of books also compounds over time, since there is so much to gain in the spaces *between* those books. Every time you read, you create fresh connections, strengthen your critical thinking skills, and create more hooks on which to hang further knowledge and understanding.

However, none of this will happen by accident. Once you make the conscious decision that you truly value reading and what it can bring to your world, then it's a question of setting up daily, automatic habits that mean you read every day almost without thinking about it. If you're starting from scratch, challenge yourself to read for just ten minutes a day (you'll need to exercise your attention and focus, too). Maintain this for a week or two and then double the time. Keep going until you are able to read with full, uninterrupted attention for an hour at a time or more.

Here are a few more ways to make sure that reading becomes your default and something you can't imagine *not* doing:

- Carry a physical book around with you at all times. You can dip into it while waiting for a bus or train, in a doctor's office, waiting for a friend, or for any spare minute when there's nothing much else to do (you know, those moments where you automatically reach for your smartphone!).
- Speaking of smartphones, they can help you: Take a good look at all the times and places in your day that you tend to reach for your phone or other device, and try to replace it with a book. If, for example, you tend to start scrolling when you get into bed in the evenings, make a habit of leaving your phone in another room and instead keep books on your bedside table.
- If you're committing to a regular daily reading block, set timers to remind you. Stack your habits by connecting reading to something else you never forget to do. For example, if you have a daily coffee and slice of toast every day before work, add a book into the routine and read while you enjoy your breakfast.

- Consider audiobooks for those times you're at the gym, shopping, commuting, or cleaning the house.
- Books are expensive, but you can find extremely cheap secondhand copies. Consider getting a library card or investigate options at a local college or university. Rare or hard-to-find books can sometimes be found on archive sites or as eBooks. Another option is to get social and share books with your friend group. If a particular book is expensive (some technical, academic works or out-of-print textbooks can cost hundreds), it may be worth pitching in to buy it together and taking turns to read it.

Smart Highlighting Strategies

Being committed to a consistent reading routine is one thing, but how exactly should you use that time? Descartes may have hinted at marking a book with a pencil if necessary, but today we know that annotating books well is an art all its own.

If you're like most students, you default to a predictable strategy: You sit down with a textbook and, using a colored marker or pen, you read along and highlight what seems to you to be important parts of the text. "This will be handy when I want to return to it later," you think, and never, ever return to it later, right?

Highlighting while reading is one of those automatic behaviors we all assume are useful, without ever taking the time to properly consider what it achieves. It's not that highlighting *can't* be used as a way to gain clarity, understanding, and memory, but rather that the act in itself is not magical— dragging a yellow highlighter pen over a few sentences will not automatically make that information stick in your mind.

AP psychology teacher Blake Harvard criticizes highlighting for its lack of critical thinking involvement, suggesting that **students often mistake highlighting for understanding**. Actively engaging the material in a book will often result in you highlighting it, but it doesn't follow that merely highlighting will lead to engagement.

In one study (Dunlosky 2013), researchers concluded that "most studies have shown no benefit to highlighting (as it is typically used) over and above the benefit of simply reading." Moreover, **highlighting as the sole strategy comes with an opportunity cost, as it may prevent you from engaging in more productive methods**. The trouble is if you blindly highlight and then believe that doing so means you have understood and retained the material, whereas you've only gained a superficial comprehension, if that. Highlighting can quickly become rote and passive, and you may be highlighting away with no real sense of why you're doing it and what the highlight actually means.

Despite these criticisms, some experts believe that highlighting can be a valuable learning tool, provided it's used correctly alongside other strategies. The key is to remember that highlighting is the start of your learning process and a means to an end. It's not the end and not the final outcome of our study process. That means that you should avoid looking at a colorful, highlighted page and assuming you're done!

Here are the three intelligent highlighter strategies that counter passivity and complacency while reading:

The Brain-Book-Buddy Strategy

Consider turning the highlighting practice on its head: **Instead of using markers to indicate "this is important," use them to draw attention to knowledge gaps**. Any learning strategy that consistently keeps you in your most pronounced areas of difficulty is going to feel less comfortable than one that gives you the illusion of making progress. But staying attuned to what you have yet to master is the fastest way to genuinely learn. Highlighting with this aim in mind means you have to return to marked sections and do so with a practical strategy. This makes your highlighting active and purposeful.

Follow this three-step process. You'll need a sheet of paper divided into three columns, or if necessary, three separate pieces of paper:

Step 1: Brain

First, answer test/practice questions without consulting external resources and highlight your uncertainties and knowledge gaps in green. You want to use your initial highlights to get you to think about what you know right now, where it comes from, how it all fits together, and what you are still not one hundred percent clear on.

Step 2: Book

Next, validate your answers using notes and textbooks, using the second column or piece of paper. Compare your answers with the external information and use a yellow highlighter to mark all the content that you are adding or correcting. This shows you where you have made mistakes or need to elaborate.

Step 3: Buddy

Finally, collaborate with peers, refining your answers further and highlighting any improvements in orange or pink. Naturally, this third step may not be feasible for you if you're studying alone or don't have suitable peers, but it's worth seeing if you can reach out to other students in some capacity and compare notes, literally.

This three-part strategy allows you to track your growing understanding and identify areas for improvement. When you look at all three columns/pages together, you get an overview of your emerging understanding, and the colors help you see at a glance the most crucial information (i.e., all those areas you need to reiterate, correct, or expand on). The first column gives you an idea of what you may have scored on a test without further study, while the last column lets you know what additional information you have to learn (i.e., exactly what remains). Using this method, you can keep focused on your goals and stay on track.

Creative Annotations

Highlighting is just one of many ways that you can engage with a text. There are countless ways to annotate books and articles and help you think critically about what you're actually reading. Unless you are deliberately reflecting on, processing, and engaging with what you read, the process is largely pointless. Instead, **try to see reading not as a one-way experience, but a dialogue or conversation**. It's your job to respond to what you read, to ask questions, to argue, to grab hold of interesting or confusing points, or to try to connect one thread to another.

Following Descartes's advice, first read through once to skim for a broad understanding, but don't be afraid to go back again and again to pull out key ideas and start to understand the structure of the argument holding the text together. Text annotation can get extremely creative, but the main thing to remember is that annotations are there to help you think—they are a means to an end, and not an end in themselves. That means that there's no point in seeing a cool and interesting annotation system and trying to graft it into your own reading process without considering what purpose it may serve.

Rather, **an annotation strategy should emerge organically from and be in support of *your thinking*.** If you are reading to gather a broad overview, then your annotations may take the form of quick summaries or mind maps. If you are reading to analyze and formulate your own position, then fill the margins with questions, retorts, or links to related information elsewhere. If you are reading to absorb and learn, then use symbols, codes, and little diagrams to help you synthesize the information, with mnemonics or color coding to help you make memorable categories and connections.

Try some of the following:

- Litte drawings or diagrams (don't worry if you're not artistically inclined!). For example, sketch a little heart with various markings inside it to indicate the different kinds of chemical bonds, or else draw lightning bolts or frowning faces over the

parts in a text where you disagree with the author.
- Draw lines between related ideas and concepts, and play around with using the line itself to communicate a message. For example, a dashed line can represent a vague or uncertain connection, a wavy line symbolizes a cause-and-effect relationship, and a jagged line shows that two ideas/paragraphs are at odds with one another.
- Make liberal use of color-coding but remember to stay consistent. It's almost always better to highlight less than to fill the page. For example, you might use one color for important people or theorists, another color for big ideas, and a third color for supporting arguments/premises for those big ideas.
- Use any symbols or markings that have personal significance for you—squiggles, question marks, exclamation points, stick figures, faces, stars, and so on can all draw your attention to important information in a meaningful and organic way. Heavily decorate a favorite passage, cross out sections that are irrelevant, draw rain clouds over parts you find difficult, or make your own impromptu diagrams,

flowcharts, or figures to quickly capture an idea being expressed in the text.

Student-Generated Questions

Mirjam Ebersbach is a psychology professor and researcher at the University of Kassel, and her investigations have shown that students usually overestimate how prepared they are for tests, primarily because techniques like lazy highlighting lull them into a false sense of security. "This superficial learning is promoted by the illusion of knowledge," she says, "which means that learners often have the impression after the reading of a text, for instance, that they got the message."

She suggests instead that learners use "student-generated questions" to go beyond the superficial. **Making your own questions forces you to engage with material on a different and deeper level.** Start with the simple, factual details, but don't be afraid of questions that will challenge you in more complex ways.

Remember that *all* learners should in some sense be their own teachers, not just the ones who are obviously self-guided. Imagine a wise old mentor perched on your shoulder, prompting you to dig a little deeper into what you're reading. You can really have fun with this; answer your questions but then also imagine that you're cleverly correcting the answers you give, as a teacher would. Make your own quizzes and tests, scribble questions in the margins, or pause now and then to guess what might be coming in the next paragraph and why.

Imagine that you're on a talk show, explaining a tricky concept or helping a learner one grade below you understand a concept you've now mastered. Keep challenging yourself to find new, thoughtful questions that drill down to the heart of the matter. A highlighted statement is like a stop sign for critical thought, but a good question is like a green light that encourages critical thinking to speed ahead.

Finally, one way to use questions is to regularly come up with mini hypotheses about what you read, especially before you have had a chance to delve deeply into the details. As you read, you can actively seek to confirm or refute the hypothesis—this active attitude means you're paying more attention and will retain what you learn. For example, you may do the following:

- Scan the title and subheadings of a journal article (let's say it's a medical journal, and the title is *The Importance of BRCA1 and BRCA2 Genes Mutations in Breast Cancer Development*) and then take a quick look at the diagrams and graphs.
- Pause to hypothesize what the article is about (you guess it's about these two genes and how they cause breast cancer if mutated, but wonder what else the authors might be talking about).
- Read the subheadings and consider the questions they trigger. One subheading is *The Molecular Subtypes of Breast Cancer*, and you think, "What are the subtypes? Do these types differ in the cancer development pathway? What molecules are they referring to, anyway? What does this have to do with the two genes in the title?" When you see the subheading *Global Prevalence* and see a world map with varied shading, you instantly think, "Why should breast cancer rates differ by country? Is it because of the genes they're talking about, or are there other factors?"
- Go in and start reading with all these questions priming you to look for answers. As you discover the answers, you note them down. When you're done, you read

again, perhaps this time with a better idea of the key ideas and how the overall argument is structured.
- Notice that a few of your questions are actually unanswered, however. You finish your reading by rewriting these questions at the top of the paper and highlighting them, reminding yourself to try to find the answer elsewhere. Perhaps you have a few qualms or concerns, and you note these too. Perhaps you use a dedicated highlight color to create a brief, single-sentence summary of the entire paper for later . . .

You get the idea! You may find one of these three strategies more useful than others, or you may discover that all three of them help you gain a fuller grasp of what you read. **All that matters at the end of the day is that you are actively engaging with what you read** and using that material to instigate and inspire your thinking. Your annotations need not be limited to the pages of that book alone, however; use numbers and letters to point to sections in other books, or make creative use of Post-It notes or good old-fashioned dog ears to help you see how a particular book may fit into your library as a whole, and your learning and development in general.

One learner may, for example, create a system where they challenge themselves to write a single paragraph summary of a book and write it on the first page of that book once they're finished reading. This summary may also reference a few other relevant books and end with unanswered questions or points of interest the book inspired. That means that any time you need to, you can pick that book up and remind yourself at a glance of the main value you distilled from its pages.

Later in this book we'll take another look at the importance of staying organized and keeping your materials neat and logical, but you can begin to shape a coherent, structured learning path just by the way you read and annotate.

The REAP Method

Let's see if there's a way to put some of these skills together. In Descartes's time, it might have been taken as a given that a person would spend time contemplating what they had read and reformulating their understanding in their own words, and so this was never explicitly included in his advice to aspiring readers. But us modern people may need a little more direction!

The REAP method, developed in 1976 by Marilyn Eanet and Anthony Manzo at the University of Missouri–Kansas City, is a framework that aims to cultivate active reading and improve comprehension. It involves four simple stages:

Reading: Identifying the author's ideas expressed in the text.

Encoding: Recasting the main ideas in your own words.

Annotating: Writing down annotations of key ideas or quotes (we've already covered this part).

Pondering: Reflecting on the content, writing comments, or criticisms, and discussing with others.

The REAP acronym is not so much a method in its own right as a framework to pull together separate methods. By using multiple channels of engagement with a text, you foster a deeper analysis over time. Confusion exists regarding the acronym "REAP," however, as another note-taking approach shares the same name, representing relating, extending, actualizing, and profiting. Introduced by Thomas Devine in 1987, this variant emphasizes making reading notes easier to memorize. Both methods have value—but we'll be talking about Eanet and Manzo's model here.

The REAP method is suitable for reading various fiction and non-fiction texts and is commonly used in both grade school and high school contexts. It's also sometimes used in college-level courses and university studies, particularly in humanities and social sciences, but can easily be adapted for use with lectures and presentations, especially those with argumentative or storytelling elements.

There is some evidence for the effectiveness of the REAP method in improving reading comprehension, recall, summarization skills, and group work. It does, however, require significant time, focus, and mental effort, making it less appropriate for note-taking during lectures. Like all learning methods, it's unsuitable for every topic in every instance, but one of the benefits of REAP is that it doesn't require you to know anything about the text you're reading—you can just jump right in, perhaps using a more complex reading strategy later on.

STEP 1: Read

Start by simply reading the piece. Don't overthink it—in the beginning all you need to do is get the overall gist of the text. Separately keep a sheet of paper where you note down the overall theme and topic—this will very often be a paraphrase of the title. For example, you may jot down, "The text is about several different precursors to the Industrial Revolution in Britain."

STEP 2: Encode

Next, you need to start engaging with the material by rewriting the main ideas in your own words. Of course, this may not be easy after just one quick reading, but don't worry, you'll come back to it again. Let's say you note on your piece of paper that there appears to be four main precursors according to the text, and you list them out in bullet points, such as "emerging factory technology" and "colonial markets."

STEP 3: Annotate

Consider this next step an expansion of the previous one. You want to go back to the broad themes you identified and paraphrased and see if you can say a little more about each one. You're exploring the text from a range of different perspectives, not just inspired by the structure the author has chosen for their piece, but by your own goals and what you hope to extract from the text for your own purposes. You may expand on one point, noting, "Expanding global colonies in the eighteenth century created an abundance of goods and also new markets to sell to."

According to Anthony Manzo's book on the REAP method, he recommends annotating according to a defined purpose, of which there are several. He suggests choosing at least three of the following:

Summary Annotation: A simple phrase condensing the text's main idea(s).

Telegram Annotation: A short message capturing the overall theme of the piece.

Poking Annotation: Highlighting an engaging section in order to provoke a response.

Question Annotation: Posing a main idea in the form of a question or hypothesis.

Personal View Annotation: Comparing your views and opinions to the author's (or perhaps to people mentioned by the author).

Critical Annotation: Analyzing the main idea to either support or critique it.

Contrary Annotation: Highlighting an opposing viewpoint.

Intention Annotation: Noting the author's purpose in creating the text.

Motivation Annotation: Trying to guess the author's motivation behind the writing, and considering the overall context and providence of the ideas expressed.

Discovery Annotation: Identifying practical concerns and questions that need explanation.

Creative Annotation: Exploring alternative solutions, outcomes, or interpretations.

STEP 4: Ponder

Once you've read through the piece a few times, encoded (paraphrased) it, and annotated it according to your different purposes, then you will probably find yourself developing a more nuanced view on it. It's at this stage that you're ready to begin formulating your own response and generating your own arguments about the material.

The ponder stage is all about allowing material to rest and percolate. Deliberately spend a little time mulling over questions that arose from your reading, and start to think of the deeper underlying implications. What else does this material link to? How might it fit in the field of study in general? How might it apply to you personally and the intentions and goals you have? Is there anything you feel is missing or extraneous?

Returning to our example, you may mull over the piece about the Industrial Revolution for a few days. You start to notice that although the text certainly tells you the precursors to the Industrial Revolution in Britain as recorded, what it doesn't tell you is why these things occurred in Britain and not some other place.

Though you have a greater understanding of how high wages, cheap energy, and certain historical advantages allowed the Industrial

Revolution to take place, you start to wonder if this is not merely begging the question. What were the precursors to these things, in other words? Reading about urbanization and the expansion of certain manufacturing technologies, you realize you've always just assumed that the Industrial Revolution could be "explained" by economic means or else by discrepancies in technological advancements. Yet something is nagging at you: You recall reading something a few months prior about the superiority of Chinese pottery. Why didn't the Industrial Revolution take place in China, when so much of their technology was better?

After a few days, you are following a fascinating rabbit hole: English pottery kilns, you learn, were cheap to make but very fuel inefficient, whereas the Chinese kiln design was sophisticated and efficient (it had to be, since fuel was scarce) but extremely expensive to build, so it required more labor to create them. The English, having greater access to fuel, actually had the less technologically advanced kiln, but succeeded because they could build more of them and hence have greater output. After reading and mulling over things further, you realize that it's too simplistic to say that technological advance helped drive the Industrial Revolution—rather it was a complex interplay between the *relative* prices of energy, labor, and capital that influenced how that technology was used.

Now, none of this new insight was anywhere to be found in the piece you read. But by simply pausing and giving yourself enough time to reflect, process, and draw connections, you arrive at a richer and more intelligent response to the material.

The ponder stage is sometimes about what you *don't* do. Instead of rushing on to reading the next text, just pause a while and "sleep on it." Give yourself time for things to sink in, especially if the material is complicated or multilayered. Then, when you next read something, whether it's on the same topic or something else entirely, you are already primed in new and interesting ways to receive that text on a deeper level. In our example, you will certainly be engaging with future texts on the Industrial Revolution with a new and expanded perspective.

In time, you'll realize that reading is never an exercise in mere absorption; rather, treat the things you read as an intellectual stimulus. The more you engage with that stimulus, the better.

Summary:

- Being a lifelong learner requires a consistent habit of reading. Reading is more than mere input; it's an *active* means to expand knowledge, find meaning, understand others and oneself, discover, and improve life while minimizing mistakes. Descartes's advice is to read once for the gist, read again to extract the overall structure and argument, annotate, and read once more to deepen understanding. Reading is a choice, and you can find time if you set your priorities correctly.
- Annotating books can aid comprehension, but don't default to mindless highlighting, which may lack critical thinking and proper engagement. Highlighting may also come with an opportunity cost and create a false sense of retention. Instead, try the "brain-book-buddy" system, creative annotations that genuinely mean something to you, and generating your own questions to deepen engagement with the text, rather than merely marking it and moving on.
- Try to see reading not as a one-way experience but a dialogue or conversation, and use markers to highlight knowledge gaps to return to deliberately later. Annotations should be organic and serve your unique purposes. Making your own

questions and hypotheses forces you to engage with material on a different and deeper level.
- The REAP method is a framework that aims to cultivate active reading and improve comprehension in four stages: reading, encoding, annotating, and pondering. By using multiple channels of engagement with a text, you foster a deeper analysis over time. Focus on paraphrasing, digesting, reflecting, and processing material, and not just passively reading it.
- Reading is never an exercise in mere absorption; rather, it is an intellectual stimulus that brings benefits the more we can engage with it.

Chapter 3: Sharpening Your Memory

Leanne considers herself intelligent. She enjoys her studies and feels like she has a very good grasp on the fundamentals. The problem is exams and tests; whenever Leanne finds herself facing that dreaded exam paper, her nerves get the better of her and she can't remember a thing.

Suddenly, all her intelligence and understanding fly out the window, and she does far worse on the exam than she knows she should. She believes she has a poor memory, but the truth is that Leanne's memory is just fine—her studying strategy, however, is not working for her. In this chapter, we're going to be looking at how to boost your own memory and learn to study and revise in a way that genuinely helps you retain everything you learn.

The Blurting Method

You may have encountered the concept of "blurting" on TikTok or YouTube, where it first gained prominence. Originally from the creator "Unjaded Jade," the technique seems to genuinely work for those who try it. According to Unjaded Jade, there are three parts to any revision process:

1. Understanding
2. Learning
3. Applying

Sometimes, we can get stuck on the first two levels and fail to challenge ourselves to move to the third. In other words, once we feel like we understand a topic and have learned it, we lose interest and move on. The result of this, however, can be a sense of having not quite fully absorbed the material. So how can the blurting technique help?

The process is as follows:

Step 1: You quickly review material you've already covered. These could be notes, flashcards, mind maps, or summaries you made during revision (you remembered to make them, right?).

Step 2: You turn this material into a series of prompts (not unlike creating questions, as we saw in a previous section) that trigger you to "blurt." A prompt can be a short phrase, a mathematical formula, a single word, a mnemonic, even a diagram or symbol.

Step 3: You give yourself a time limit and start the clock. You may have to experiment with a good time period. Start with around three or four minutes for a standard textbook chapter, but use your discretion to dial this up or down as needed. Put the pressure on but remember you don't need to make it a race.

Step 4: With the timer running, quickly move through each of your prompts and get ready to blurt! This just means throwing out any and all ideas that spring to mind when you see this prompt. Until the timer runs out, just do a kind of "brain dump" and dig around in your memory for everything you already know about this topic. You could do this verbally, but it may make more sense to quickly scribble notes on a blank piece of paper just so you have a record of what you came up with.

Step 5: When time's up, consult the material you started with. It's now time to annotate these notes and mark all those areas where you're missing knowledge and struggling, as well as places you've mastered well. Use your chosen or preferred annotation system to really keep things coherent—for example, a red marker to draw attention to knowledge gaps.

Keen readers will notice that Jade's blurting technique is actually a modified form of "testing" or relearning that we explored in the very first chapter. When you deliberately practice recalling previously absorbed material, you are in essence testing yourself. It is a way to make sure you are taking that crucial third step, applying, and not staying stuck in the first two stages of more abstract/hypothetical understanding.

Incorporating the blurting method may initially seem like hard work. It takes far more brainpower to put yourself on the spot in this way and force a response without the crutch of notes or books. Blurting, however, is so effective that it may end up saving you time in the long run. You will quickly identify areas that need improvement and channel your energy there, rather than wasting time and falsely believing that you have retained material when really, you have only understood and learned it—i.e., you have step 1 and 2 but *not* step 3.

One way to incorporate this method into your study routine is to use it as a kind of bookend. For example, start every study block with a quick blurting session. Settle on a few prompts that quickly trigger you to recall whatever you can from the previous study block. This quickly lets you know what you need to focus on in the remainder of the study session—i.e., your knowledge gaps. At the end of that study block, do a quick blurting session once more and compare your notes. Have you improved?

When used this way, blurting brings some helpful structure to your goals and, in the long term, gives you a clear picture of your progress over time. You not only stay focused and effective, but you keep your motivation up since you are clearly able to see results even from one session to another.

A few things to bear in mind when trying this approach:

Consider Mixing Written and Verbal Blurting

Saying out loud everything you can recall has the advantage of being quick, but of course you lose the ability to produce a written record. Choose an approach that best fits your topic and unique goals, but consider a blend of both verbal and written. Most students understand that there's value in varying the format of their study material (for example, audio, written, diagrams, etc.), but few pay attention to their *output*. You may uncover additional corners of understanding if you practice blurting both out loud and in written forms—or even consider blurting out sketches and diagrams, if appropriate. Some students might like to blurt out loud and record themselves, then return to these recordings later.

Remind Yourself that You Are Not Grading Your Knowledge

There is no element of judgment or appraisal in the blurting process. That means there's no point in getting discouraged if you can't think of much, or triumphant because you can recall a lot. The point, in fact, is not to get it perfect. Rather, the exercise will yield valuable data no matter what. If you can't think of much, well, that's useful data because it means you've ascertained a baseline level against which to compare future progress, and identified a direction for improvement. If you can think of a lot, that's useful data too, because it suggests that it may be time to move on to something a little more challenging.

Just remember not to panic or get down on yourself for not doing as well as you thought you might. The first time you try this method, you may be surprised at just how large the discrepancy is between what you thought you had retained and what you have actually retained! Don't worry, it's normal and all the more reason to stick with the method to improve.

Be Mindful of the Prompts You're Using

You may need to experiment a little with these. Take inspiration from actual test material you're likely to encounter in the future, or else make it an exercise in itself to create questions and triggers that directly challenge your weak points. Done correctly, compiling a set of prompts is itself an illuminating exercise. Just remember to keep things varied and genuine.

You don't want to merely teach yourself to respond in a rote way to a predictable trigger that doesn't really reflect the kind of test situation you may encounter in real life. In other words, don't fall into the trap of happily practicing a set of easy skills you're not actually required to have!

Combine Blurting with Interleaving Practice

Recall that interleaving is about mixing a variety of topics, materials, and prompts in a single study session. Though it may feel extremely challenging at first, experiment with mixing up prompts from different sources in one blurting session. Your brain will have to work extra hard to quickly recall and respond. This is excellent practice not just for more complex exams and tests, but for real life, where problems are seldom presented to you in a neat, predictable format that you've already rehearsed.

Don't Cheat!

This goes without saying, but try to remind yourself that the goal is not to "get the answer right." Rather, you want to get an accurate sense of your current recall and retention, and you can only do that by being really honest with yourself. Either you can remember the information or you can't. There's no point in quickly sneaking a peek of the textbook to remind yourself—rather, note that you can't remember, and move on. No hints, excuses, or justifications.

The more accurate you can be during the revision process, the more accurate your final output will be later on. So, for example, if you're revising vocabulary words for a second language, don't go too easy on yourself and honestly mark instances where you've gotten the spelling wrong. Make a clear note of this and make sure that you remember it for next time, rather than shrugging and thinking, "Well, the spelling is *almost* right. That's good enough." In an exam situation, the marker won't be taking that attitude!

Other Ways to Use Blurting

You can incorporate "mini blurts" into a single study session by challenging yourself to quickly blurt what you know after every ten minutes of a lecture, after every paragraph or handful of pages, or after every new chunk or unit in the study material. You can do this really quickly—just close the book, pause the video or look away from the page for a moment, and ask your brain to quickly blurt out everything it can recall from the last few minutes or so. Depending on how this goes, you could choose to re-read or re-listen, make a quick summary, jot down a question to investigate later, or annotate your text if you've uncovered an idea you wish to draw attention to.

Another thing to consider is that it may be worthwhile to try not blurting immediately after you take in some new material. Why? If you're reading a paragraph, for example, and you challenge yourself to immediately remember what you read, your working memory can easily step in to help you do this. However, this form of memory is different from long-term memory, which you would strengthen by asking your brain to recall information after more time has passed. Play around with the period of time you wait before prompting a blurt, from immediately to within the same hour-long study session, to days and even weeks between.

Give your brain plenty of time to rest between blurting sessions. This approach should be thought of a little like sprinting—it's intense but short, and there's no need to prolong things to get results. You probably know this already, but your learning will always be optimized when you pay attention to your physical and psychological well-being, too. Stay healthy, get plenty of sleep, and make good use of breaks to rest and consolidate all the hard work you're asking your memory to do for you.

Finally, you can use a form of blurting when in a real exam situation, too. This works particularly well for longer question formats and essays. First read the question, take a deep breath, then quickly blurt out everything you immediately think of on a separate piece of paper. Do a memory dump and get it all out— you can then comb through these notes and craft a more deliberate answer. This method is great for keeping you focused and organized, but it also calms your nerves since often students are worried they'll forget something important.

The Power of Memory Anchors

Let's return to Leanne and her belief that she was simply born with a terrible memory. What *is* memory, anyway, and how does it work?

You can think of memory as a kind of neural habit—a connection between your nerve cells that has been created and then strengthened over time, until that connection can be made easily. In the past, people tended to think of memories as *things*—mental items that could be stored in the brain like books on a bookshelf. A more useful way to think about it, however, is to imagine that a **memory is an action** in the same way a bicep curl is an action. When your arm is at rest, there is no bicep curl. The more repetitions of bicep curls you do, however, the more those particular muscles strengthen, and the easier it is to do bicep curls on demand in the future.

It's the same with memory. Every time you recall a memory, your neurons are doing one "rep." The more reps you do, the stronger your memory, and the easier it is to recall. Memory underpins all our learning. If you think about all the things you know today (including things like how to walk, how to speak a language, how to read and write, and how to count), they all began as unknowns to you and gradually became cemented enough in your mental wiring that they were automatic and took no effort at all.

It's worth reminding yourself of all the things you already have successfully memorized the next time you suppose you have a "bad memory" like Leanne. It may be more accurate to say that we all have good memories; we are just more or less effective at using those memories.

Neuroscientists today agree that when it comes to memory optimization, three things matter most:

1. Repetition
2. Consolidation
3. Testing

Behind every successful memory is **repetition**—lots of repetition. A young child may repeat hundreds of thousands of words and sentences in a single year before their speaking practice yields results. By the time they're an adult, speaking is automatic and they have no trouble recalling thousands and thousands of vocabulary words. Remember the "forgetting curve"? The more times we revisit a memory, and the more that memory is tested through deliberate recall, the more it is consolidated in our brains. But there is another aspect to how memories are formed, and understanding this aspect can help us improve our own strategy. The aspect is **anchoring**.

Consider this example: You're walking in a mall one day and a sales assistant spritzes you with a scent as you walk by. All at once, and entirely without your conscious will, your mind explodes with several closely associated memories. You instantly think of someone you used to date in college ten years ago, someone who used to wear that fragrance; instantly you see their face again, you can hear all the things they used to say in their unique voice, and your mind conjures up several specific scenes, moments, places, and ideas. You didn't have to do anything to get all these memories to come back to you—they just did. They were triggered by that single stimulus of the familiar fragrance.

Wouldn't it be amazing if you could remember *everything* just as easily?

We can call the distinctive fragrance in this example a "memory anchor." The reason it's so easy to recall memories that are anchored this way is that they are so firmly embedded in our embodied experience via our senses.

Your brain evolved to help you survive and thrive in the world—a world that is rich and full of varied stimuli. Memory helps us learn and adapt to this vivid environment, and so information is never encoded in isolation, but rather as complex networks of associations. When you sit down to study a sequence of facts from a textbook, in other words, this is precisely the *opposite* of the way your memory evolved to function best.

When you smell a familiar fragrance, you activate a whole network of neural associations that came along with the experience the first time you encoded it to memory. Who wore it, how you felt when you first smelled it, the place you were, the sensations in your body, and so on. Later, the fragrance acts like a trigger and activates that entire network of connections so that a flood of memories becomes accessible to you. If we use this principle deliberately and create memories that are multisensory and rich, then we give ourselves multiple "handles" with which to retrieve memories—like making sure we have many different threads to pull on to activate that network.

Try to embed your learning in the real world, which means connecting your experiences to as many sources of data from your *sense organs* as possible. Actively try to link up stimuli across your senses of sight, hearing, touch, taste, and smell. Extending this principle, also consider imbuing memories with real meaning and significance—i.e., by adding emotional content, context, and logical consequence (more on that later).

Memory anchoring is a technique for boosting retention because it works *with* the brain's natural memory mechanisms. You don't need to force yourself to memorize by rote or sheer willpower, but merely learn to use the ability of your brain to naturally make associations across a range of different neural channels. What's more, when we anchor new material to material we have already learned and memorized, those connections are all the more robust.

A great principle to remember is: **How you think about something is how you'll remember something. The way a memory is made determines the way it is recalled later on.**

How do we actually apply memory anchoring in real life? Let's look at an example. Imagine you're studying for a chemistry exam one day. You have four chapters to learn for a test, and so you decide to study each chapter in a different room of your house. Not only that, but when you study, you use a different set of markers and take the time to set different "scenes" at each study session—you eat a specific snack and wear a particular outfit, for example. You take care to notice all the tiny details in your environment as you learn (not to mention all the colorful annotating and note-taking you're doing).

When the time comes to take your chemistry exam, you feel prepared. You recognize that a particular question is asking about Chapter 3, which you remember tackling in your bedroom. Instantly, it's as though you're right there in the bedroom again—you can remember the time of day and the warmth of the light coming through the bedroom window (touch), you can remember the scent of coffee in the next room (smell), that you were wearing your favorite yellow pajamas (sight), that a bee flew in the window, and that you could hear Elton John's "Candle in the Wind" being played somewhere in the distance (sound).

Painting a picture this way helps you remember the entire scene. Then, you start to remember more details from your study session—the exercises you did, the notes you made. By linking all this sensory data, your memories become more real and anchored in reality, and thus easier to recall.

How to Anchor into Meaning

In the previous example, sensory data was used as a memory anchor. There are also other ways, however, to create and use such anchors, and one way is to deliberately create networks of **meaning**.

Let's say that as you study Chapter 3 in the chemistry textbook, you start to tell yourself a little story about an important chemical reaction that you'll be tested on. In your story, the element sulfur is like a wicked witch character in a fairy tale, and she reacts violently to all oxidizing agents, like peroxide. You cast peroxide as a beautiful blonde princess (just like Princess Diana, whom Elton John once sang the song "Candle in the Wind" for—another great anchor).

Your links and associations are not just superficial, however. You can easily imagine this princess being blonde (yellow?) because "peroxide" is a term that makes you think of bleaching at a hair salon. But you deliberately make your connections more meaningful than this. An oxidizing agent oxidizes other substances, which means it makes that substance lose electrons—in your story, the beautiful princess "steals" these electrons from the wicked witch sulfur, and in doing so takes her yellowness and keeps it for herself, which explains why she's blonde . . . Not only does this little tale cement the relationship between blondeness, yellowness, sulfur, princesses, and so on, but it draws attention to a genuine reality of chemistry that you are trying to learn and memorize—i.e., the reaction between sulfur and peroxide itself.

All these details are a little silly, but their silliness means they stick with you, and you soon build a web that is easy to pull on the next time you need to recall information about sulfur, its characteristics, and the way it reacts to peroxide. Now, when you head into the exam room, let's say you see the phrase "oxidizing agents" in a question. This word alone instantly makes you think of peroxide and blondeness and the song and how sulfur reacts violently, etc. All the information comes flooding back to you . . . without you needing to anxiously wrack your brain. In fact, used this way, it almost feels like your memory could have infinite capacity!

Why Mnemonics Don't Always Work

Most of us have been taught a few mnemonics in school—i.e., all those little verbal tricks to help us quickly remember strings of information. A dictionary definition tells us that a mnemonic is

> "a device such as a pattern of letters, ideas, or associations that assists in remembering something. For example, *Richard Of York Gave Battle In Vain* for the colors of the spectrum (red, orange, yellow, green, blue, indigo, violet)."

Though the concept of a mnemonic makes a certain sense, the fact is that you're simply asking your brain to remember something else—and this thing is often even less meaningful or embedded in reality. Who, for instance, can easily remember "Richard of York" unprompted, and are they really likely to remember this quite odd sentence with any more ease than they could simply recall the image of a rainbow and how the colors are likely to be arranged?

Mnemonics are useful, but they are limited. For example, you could certainly learn the mnemonic "My Very Excellent Mom Just Served Us Noodles" to help you remember the names and order of the planets in the solar system, but how on earth will you remember the mnemonic itself? Especially given that excellent moms and noodles have precisely nothing to do with planets?

Mnemonics often fail because they lack any real meaning and logic—which is what your brain relies on to make those vital associations that form the foundation of your memory. You need to make more meaningful connections, not fewer. The connections need to mirror the way you're actually thinking about the topic at hand.

Consider an updated version to remember the order and names of planets: "My Very Easy Memory Jingle Seems Useful Naming Planets." This one is slightly better because it refers to planets and memory, so it has a greater chance of being recalled should you find yourself thinking, "How am I going to remember the planets?" It can even be changed to "My Very Easy Memory Jingle Seems Useless Now" to reflect that Pluto is no longer considered a planet—an extra layer of meaning!

But we can take this further still. Let's return to our complicated story about peroxide and sulfur from the previous example. The tale was memorable because it *meant* something. It turned a dry, abstract equation into a story—and your brain is far, far better at remembering stories than strings of boring data.

In fact, you can test this out right now for yourself. Without going back to the text to re-read it, see if you can recall right now the details of the story of the chemistry exam. Try to remember not only the details of the bedroom and how it felt to study Chapter 3 on that warm day, but also see what you can remember about the reaction between peroxide and sulfur.

What details from the studying scene did you find easiest to recall? The yellow pajamas? The bee flying in the window? The song?

And which feature from the chemical reaction story stuck out most to you?

The details you remembered most clearly were probably those you had the strongest emotional reaction to.

Perhaps you could clearly see the yellow pajamas in your mind's eye because you have a similar pair yourself, or you remembered the bit about Princess Diana because you still have a memory of seeing news of her death on TV so many years ago. Not only do all these connections link up with one another, but they link up with pre-existing knowledge, too.

Let's imagine you were faced right now with a question from a chemistry paper that went like this:

What does an oxidizing agent do?

   a) It's a substance in a redox chemical reaction that receives electrons from another substance
   b) It's a substance in a redox chemical reaction that donates electrons to another substance
   c) It catalyzes redox reactions
   d) None of the above

Now, if you can remember the story detail about the princess who "steals" yellowness from sulfur (i.e., electrons), you can probably reason your way to the correct option (it's A). You can only answer this question, however, because your story goes beyond being a mere mnemonic and makes real, meaningful connections that exist in the real world.

Anchoring in meaning is about finding ways to *logically and meaningfully* connect ideas in a way that reflects their true connection in real life—something mnemonics often cannot do. Let's say instead of making your own story, you rely on a common mnemonic designed to help chemistry students remember details about redox reactions. The mnemonic is: "LEO the lion says GER." This helps you remember that "loss of electrons is oxidation, and gain of electrons is reduction." That's all well and good, and this trick may help you answer the above question . . . if you can remember the mnemonic, that is.

The trouble is that this mnemonic doesn't fit in anywhere—there are too few sensory anchors, and it doesn't connect to any network of information we already possess. Most of us have little experience with lions, and nothing at all to spontaneously prompt us to think about them. Thus, we risk ending up in the same position as Leanne. She may have a head full of mnemonics, but none of them connect to anything, and none of them mean anything. This feels, as she says, like her mind has "gone blank."

Summary:

- The study process consists of understanding, learning, and applying—unless you apply what you learn, your retention and memory won't reach its full potential.
- In the blurting process, we revise material, create prompts and questions, and then practice "dumping" everything we know in limited time without outside help. This improves recall and alerts us to knowledge gaps so we can revise further with purpose. Blurting can bring structure and focus to your study and help you track progress. Blurting can be written, verbal, or a blend of both.
- Use a variety of prompts, be honest but nonjudgmental with yourself, and don't cheat. The goal is not to "get the answer right" but rather to gain an accurate sense of your current recall and retention, and then take action accordingly.
- Memory can be thought of as a kind of neural habit—a connection between your

nerve cells that has been created and then strengthened over time. Memory is an action. When it comes to memory optimization, three things matter most: repetition, consolidation, and testing.
- Anchoring is one way we can drastically improve retention. By creating and tapping into networks of neural associations from sensory data, we can improve our memory. Make learning multisensory, connect it to what you already know, and imbue it with meaning and emotion to enhance recall. The way a memory is made determines the way it is recalled later on.
- Mnemonics often don't work because they are not sufficiently imbued with meaning or have only a superficial connection to real relationships in the world. Use stories, metaphors, and analogies that are logically meaningful.

Chapter 4: Be Strategic; Stay Organized

Daniel is making strides in his learning journey. He's found a great rhythm using the STIC framework and has developed a consistent flow between testing, spaced/interleaved practice, and plenty of smart note-taking. He is learning to be his own teacher and gently scaffolding his way to more advanced understanding, dialing up the challenge, and adjusting his goals as he goes along. He reads daily and produces countless annotated texts, summaries, mind maps, and blurting notes to guide his process.

This is actually his problem, however—he is drowning in notes. Daniel is extremely motivated and not afraid of working hard, but he falls short when it comes to keeping himself organized. He is starting to notice that merely looking at his cluttered and chaotic study room is making him want to procrastinate.

We mentioned earlier that the best way to learn is to work with all the brain's innate powers and preferences so that we develop in a natural way. The same is true when it comes to organization; **our outside is a reflection of our inside, and the degree of organization and logic in our external world mirrors the degree of organization in our internal world**. Change one and you cannot help but change the other. That's why in this chapter we'll be looking at ways to use principles of organizing not just to stay neat and tidy, but to improve the *quality of your thought* more generally.

The Zettelkasten Method

You've highlighted all the interesting bits in a text and made a useful summary . . . but what do you do with the paper itself *and* the additional summary you've generated?

You've made a comprehensive study timetable and scheduled all your learning blocks . . . but where should this schedule live?

You've collected an impressive array of books, papers, and journal articles . . . but what on earth are you going to do to stop them from proliferating in piles all over your desk?

The answer to all these problems, of course, is to have a clear and intelligent system of organization.

The Zettelkasten method is one such system, and it should not be thought of as an organization or tidying approach, but rather **a method for more disciplined and effective thinking.**

It's more than just Marie Kondo for your office; it's an organizational framework that helps you process and manage information of all types so that your process—whatever it is—remains as streamlined and effective as possible. By creating such an external storage system, you relieve the burden on your own memory and actually enhance your recall abilities. By keeping your system logical, meaningful, and relevant, you create more robust mental models within your own brain. Finally, a good system like the Zettelkasten method is also a clever way to cut down on stress and overwhelm so you feel more in charge and in control . . . and less likely to procrastinate or make preventable mistakes.

Any organization system has to do one thing well: **help you connect.** It needs to systematically link ideas together so that you can easily find them again, but also inspire you to make fresh connections, solve problems, or uncover new, interesting relationships you didn't see before. Such a system can, if done correctly, act as a kind of secondary brain.

"Zettelkasten" is simply German for "note box" and refers to a collection of filed index cards or sticky notes that point to other pieces of information. These notes can be categorized and organized in a meaningful way to express relationships and higher-order concepts, a little like creating real-life "hyperlinks" or materially representing a "train of thought."

The method was introduced by sociologist and prolific scholarly author Niklas Luhmann. Having written more than four hundred journal articles and seventy books, the man clearly required a data management system to keep track of everything! He is said to have created almost one hundred thousand individual index notes in his own Zettelkasten. Luhmann's goal was to consistently connect every new piece of information he gathered to knowledge he had already banked, creating vast idea webs. In some ways, what Luhmann did was create his own unique and personalized pre-internet version of Wikipedia.

How can you create your own Zettelkasten?

A few points before we explore the step-by-step process:

- Your system will not necessarily look like anyone else's, so don't worry too much about mimicking other people's approaches. Your system will be effective to the degree it serves *your* organizational needs and goals.
- Be patient. A working system will take time to grow—it is not something you can create to completion overnight.
- By that same token, expect that your system will be constantly changing as you edit, update, add, and remove pieces of information. This is a feature of the method, not a flaw.
- Keep things as simple as they can possibly be. You don't want to give yourself more work!

- Be creative. You can include pictures, images, and symbols in your notes if you like, and you can experiment with all kinds of digital note-keeping systems, too.

Before we move on, let's consider the *types* of information you can record in your system:

1. Literature notes
2. Reference notes
3. Permanent notes
4. Fleeting notes

Each note serves a specific purpose (if it doesn't serve a purpose that you can see, it shouldn't be a note!).

Literature notes are produced when you're reading and want to keep a record of specific information—for example, new vocabulary words, summaries, questions, links to other related works, personal reactions to the text, comments, instructions to follow up on, or sample test prompts and questions. This will be closely connected to your annotation technique.

Make sure you're creating high-quality notes that future you will be able to understand: Write legibly, include page numbers and dates, for example, and give enough context so that you know exactly why you thought this information was important.

Reference notes are produced when you are trying to group or categorize information. Referencing means that a piece of information connects somehow to a bigger topic of discussion elsewhere—the reference note tells you where a piece of data belongs and why. For example, if you're doing research for a dissertation, you may mark certain readings and diagrams with a label/tag that shows that they belong to certain main sections of your thesis.

Color coding is also a way to create a reference note, as is using special numbers or shorthand that you can then later search, such as gathering up everything that you've tagged with yellow marker so that you can start synthesizing disparate bits and pieces into a coherent essay. Most of us will have overlapping reference points—for example, a single "zettel" (note) is cross-referenced with four or five different topics.

Permanent notes are standalone and made without such context or external reference. These include random thoughts that occurred to you, summaries, new ideas and possibilities. These are the permanent nodes in your knowledge web—the things that stay relatively the same.

Fleeting notes are quickly jotted down to capture all those ideas that strike you spontaneously. They are necessarily unstructured and spur-of-the-moment, and you will need to process them more fully at some point, either discarding them or transforming them into something more useful. Fleeting notes can also be thought of as mere reminders or placeholders. They are temporary and need to be "tidied up" every once in a while.

Step 1: Read and take intelligent annotated notes

We've already discussed some options for creating truly useful notes, so we won't reiterate those methods here. Just remember to choose an annotating strategy that earns its keep and genuinely makes your life easier.

Example: You're doing research for a novel you are writing set in 1883 in the Wild West. You're systematically reading through a collection of history books written on this period and marking all those sections and ideas that most relate to the story you want to write.

Step 2: Process these notes into a "zettel"

Once you've done your reading and/or created notes, you need to make an index card for your Zettelkasten. This can be done with paper and pen, or digitally using any one of the many available apps and software tools designed for this purpose. Try to keep things as simple and streamlined as possible.

Example: After you finish each Wild West history book, you create a single card that contains key data about the book itself (the author, the book's main idea, most useful pages/chapters, and the big ideas you've extracted from that book).

You may find yourself creating subcategories of index cards depending on the complexity of your information. For example, one book may have focused on clothing and fashion during the period, but you have teased out a few subthemes such as the class implications of different styles of dress, the availability of certain materials given manufacturing limitations at the time, culture standards of modesty, and how clothing was laundered, especially in desert towns where water was scarce.

Step 3: Create links

You need to deliberately create structure and draw relationships between each of these cards.

Maybe you assign each main theme of your book an ID tag and a letter, and design a filing system where every subcategory gets a number, too. You could follow this with more numbers that point to smaller subcategories—for example, the ID tag "C-2-51" could indicate the main topic of clothing (the letter C), the subcategory of historical materials (number 2), and the exact data card in that category (for instance, an important statistic about the economic viability of flax and linen at the time, represented by the number 51).

As you can see, **it's not enough to simply create a note**. **The note only comes alive when it is fully and meaningfully integrated into the bigger whole.** You need to have both the fine detail and the bigger overview to prevent yourself from getting "lost in the weeds" or distracted. In some cases, your filing system can actually help you stay focused and on track. In our example, you may go down a rabbit hole reading more and more about flax and linen, but quickly start to lose sight of your main goals. Realizing how difficult it is to integrate such material into your existing web gives you the hint that you've strayed off course and gets you refocused again.

Step 4: Continuously review

Merely having created a knowledge network is not the same as being intelligent. Again, the network is only useful to the extent that it's actually used. Returning to an earlier metaphor, simply having strong bicep muscles doesn't mean much in and of itself—the value comes from *using* those muscles. In the same way, a perfect Zettelkasten system that sits on a bookshelf does not serve much of a purpose other than to perhaps make you feel accomplished.

Instead, think of such a system as a living dynamic tool that works hard for you. To make the best use of your notes, actively review and amend them over time. You could potentially use your notes as prompts for blurting practice, or as tools to help you structure your own study sessions, revise, or even create new patterns and connections.

In the example of writing a Western novel, you may discover over time that merely writing things down changes the way you think about certain ideas; by putting specific concepts next to each other, your creativity is stimulated, and you may even see new solutions to old problems.

Perhaps you notice that there is in fact a significant overlap in the data you're gathering about Wild West fashions and the manufacturing processes that supported their production. Not only are you able to add realistic and historically accurate details about clothing at the time, but you also have a flash of insight into a potential plot development that you hadn't considered before . . . perhaps something to do with sabotage and intrigue at a flax mill in a dangerous frontier town in Salt Lake City.

Step 5: Make it part of your workflow

The main risk with the Zettelkasten method is that you lose momentum and forget to keep it updated, allowing it to wither away and be forgotten. To avoid this, make sure that you're building in a little scheduled time every few days to tend to your system. For example, you could spend an hour or so every week updating your system and using the process to guide the coming week's goals and consolidate the activities and information from the week past.

The very moment you come across something useful, seize it, either making a zettel immediately or creating notes that you can later transform into a zettel. **Ask yourself where this piece of information belongs, what category it fits, what problem it solves, or what topic it relates to, then tag and file it accordingly.**

Let's say you're casually reading a newspaper one day and come across a story about the earliest founding families who settled in Salt Lake City. You clip the article and keep it somewhere safe so that at the end of the week, when you're reviewing and updating your notes, you can process it properly. Knowing that there is always a dedicated time and place to incorporate every new piece of knowledge means that nothing potentially useful gets past you.

The "Dump, Lump, and Jump" Technique

If you're someone whose learning is focused primarily on *creation*, then the Zettelkasten approach (which is more suited for research and academic study) may not be the neatest fit. A simpler and potentially more useful approach is called "lump, dump, and jump," and comes from prolific content creator and organizational guru Aidan Helfant from aidanhelfant.com. It would work well for the person wanting to take notes from the Zettelkasten system and use them to inspire the creation of new material (for example, a Western novel!).

Helfant describes the following process for coming up with dozens and dozens of blog posts, course materials, newsletters, essays, and so on. The process is simple:

Step 1: Dump

This is not dissimilar to the blurting concept. Just dump out every idea or piece of data you can think of in response to a particular prompt. Do this without second-guessing or judging yourself—just put *everything* down.

Step 2: Lump

Now sift through what you've set down and try to categorize everything into related groups and themes. This will later become the outline for the thing you're trying to create—for example, an essay or blog post.

Step 3: Jump

Cut and paste your categorized notes into a document. Now, you have a framework to write around—and you'll also be able to clearly see if there are any gaps in the logic or missing pieces requiring further research.

In our example, the above work process could be used to transform all the historical notes you've gathered into coherent chapters. You take each category or note and work through the process of dump, lump, and jump to create a unique chapter that brings together everything you've collected and synthesized.

Create a Skill Tree

In the Zettelkasten system, you're teaching yourself a sophisticated way of keeping track of data and linking ideas together to enhance your recall and understanding. But of course, not everyone's learning journey is about *information*—sometimes, it's about *skills*. In this chapter, we'll consider how to manage and organize your development of a particular skill, namely by learning to connect it to other skills (are you noticing a theme yet?).

The creation of a skill tree can help you better master a skill since it requires that you break down the overall skill into a set of smaller subskills. Not only does this give you a better visual grasp of everything you're required to master, but it also gives you a framework for structuring your goals and your learning process in general.

The skill tree concept will be pretty familiar to gamers since these are common in various RPG games like *Diablo 2*. In this game, for example, every character is given a skill tree that explains their unique areas of mastery, so you can see at a glance their particular areas of mastery and how those areas relate to one another.

The point of laying out skills in this way rather than having them merely listed is to show the hierarchy and how certain skills have other skills as prerequisites. For example, certain abilities and advancements are only "unlocked" once other achievements have been reached.

Skill trees reflect the actual nature of developing mastery in the real environment—sometimes, you may even require a set of proficiencies from some separate branch. Just as knowledge, facts, and data can be best acquired by constructing meaningful and logical mental webs, skills and abilities can be mapped in the same way. You may have also noticed that doing so is a natural way to practice the art of scaffolding and maintain your learning within your personal "zone of proximal development."

There are three main purposes behind building a skill tree:

1. **Increase self-awareness**. You gain clarity not just on your current skill level, but also about where you need to be. This enables meaningful tracking and monitoring.

2. **Increase focus**. By setting your skills out in a hierarchy, you can clearly understand which need to be tackled first, and adjust your efforts and attention accordingly. You avoid wasting time attempting things prematurely, or needlessly covering old ground.
3. **Increase purposiveness**. A skill tree quickly becomes a map and plan. It will help you identify exactly what resources, materials, and exercises you need to be focusing on at each step of the journey.

Education writer, entrepreneur, and editor for SkillUp, Danny Forest shares a simple example of what a skill tree looks like:

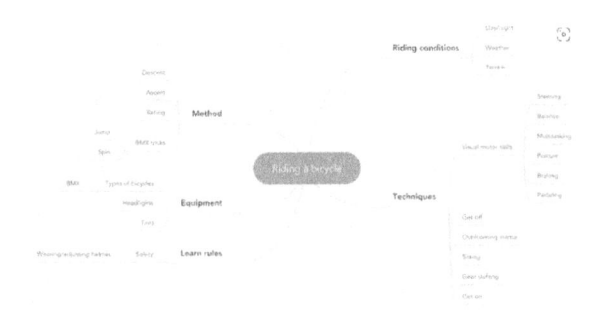

This diagram contains three levels that delineate the "subskills" required for learning to ride a bike. One thing that might immediately occur to you on looking at this skill tree is that there is obviously some leeway in how you decide to construct it. For example, you may think that there are a few skills missing, or that some are really variations of the same skill, or else you may disagree on the categorization of a skill and how it relates to others above/below it.

This is worth considering: **The value of a skill tree depends heavily on how well it's constructed**. In fact, putting together a skill tree can be a learning opportunity in itself since it will force you to very carefully spell out what you're intending to learn. That said, your skill tree may look different from someone else's purely because their goals and intentions are different. For example, learning to cycle for fun is different from learning to cycle in order to commute to work, or even because you want to learn to do mountain biking or races. What matters is that the map you draw for yourself is able to help you successfully acquire the skill you want, given your goals.

Skills are literal neural connections in your brain. Every skill you possess is a composite of many other skills chunked together. Even a "simple" skill like walking requires several other subskills:

- Standing
- Balancing upright
- Raising the legs
- Bending the knees
- Calculating distance and force
- Adjusting to varying surfaces
- Swinging the arms

Now, if you wanted to run, you'd need to master all the above skills required for walking first before attempting all the additional skills required to run. If you wanted to do marathon running, you'd need to build even more skills onto the running framework. You could also transfer some of these skills to other tasks like dancing or jumping, and then those could in turn be transferred to things like playing certain sports.

The "SkillUp tree principle" acknowledges these interconnected skill chunks and guides your learning in a logical way. Consider that not everyone will be attempting a new task with the same set of banked skills!

The idea is to purposefully connect the skills you already have to the ones you're

trying to acquire—i.e., to cultivate connected skills. To properly learn a skill, you need to really understand all the ingredients that go into making up that skill, and in what order. Once you've built a few skills, you can start chunking them together, and once you've mastered a particular chunk, you can extend that learning to another skill in just the same way as you'd learn to walk, then run, then dance.

Now, all of this may seem pretty obvious, but when you try it for yourself in your own life and with a topic that is a little more complex than riding a bike or walking, you'll see just how useful it can be. Often, we fail to make progress in our learning and development not because we lack intelligence or discipline, but because we lack strategy. For example, we may force ourselves to try to master a skill that is made up of separate components we actually haven't mastered yet. We may get frustrated and start to believe that the task is too difficult or that we lack ability—which means we risk giving up prematurely.

When faced with a new skill, we often only see the total, final product of many years of learning. This can conceal the fact that **learning a skill is a multistep process**. For example, we see a gymnast performing a complicated move on the bar and wrongly assume that this is just a single skill, whereas it's really the culmination of very many separate skills, each of which was mastered in due course at the right time. The gymnast had to work hard at balance, muscle control, alignment, and all the separate movements that go toward creating the maneuver you observed.

Finally, one important insight that can be gained from working with skill trees is to make better use of what you already know how to do. Sometimes, when people become committed to personal development projects, they get stuck "reinventing the wheel" and remain perpetual beginners with vastly different skills that don't relate at all to one another. Maybe they take up chess, and then they do horseback riding, and then they learn a programming language, and then they learn French.

There's nothing at all wrong with doing this, especially if you derive real enjoyment from the process. You will not need to start from scratch each time, however, if you build intelligently on your existing skill set. For example, you know how to ride a bike, so you challenge yourself to learn how to ride a motorbike, and then you start wondering about riding a horse (is riding a horse anything like riding a bike? Compile a skill tree and see for yourself!).

Over time, you will build a connected web of linked skills, all of which are mutually reinforcing. This will be ultimately far more robust than picking up several unconnected skill sets here and there.

How to Build a High-Quality Skill Tree

Step 1. List the concepts, facts, and procedures

In the bestseller *Ultralearning: Accelerate Your Career, Master Hard Skills and Outsmart the Competitio*n, author Scott H. Young outlines some important terms that can help you construct your skill tree:

Concepts: These are things that you need to understand.

Facts: These are things that you need to memorize.

Procedures: These are things that you need to practice.

Create a list of these three and write them down on a piece of paper divided into three columns:

Concepts	Facts	Procedures

Step 2. Construct the tree

For Forest, a skill tree typically follows this format:

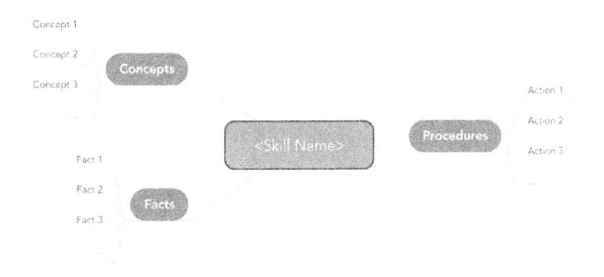

To keep going with the bike-riding example, he explains how a skill tree can be constructed using your identified concepts, facts, and procedures (the latter being put on the right side):

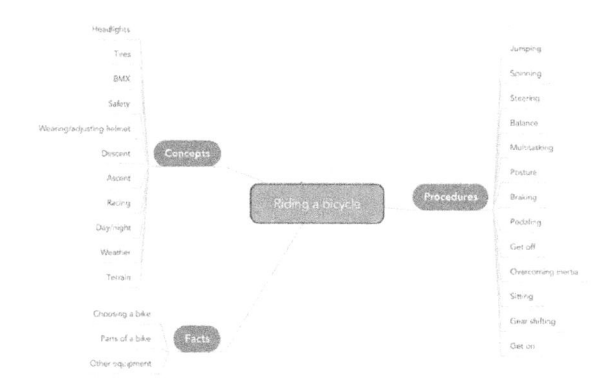

Step 3. Assess your current proficiency

When you can't think of anything more to add to the tree, go back and look at each part and rate your own current skill level. Don't worry if it's low across the board—that's normal for a brand-new skill. Try to stay consistent in how you grade yourself, and use a ranking system such as the following:

0 = You know absolutely nothing

1 = You're a beginner

2 = You're pretty good

3 = You're very good

4 = You know all there is to know

For some skills, this may not be adequate, and you'll need to extend your range a little, but don't overthink it. The main goal is just to identify your starting point so that you can meaningfully tell when you've improved.

Step 4: Learn the skills

Once you've gained awareness of what you're trying to learn, the next step will become obvious to you. Schedule it in and get to work acquiring that next step. Then, come back to your original skill tree and see where your new competence places you.

You can also use this tree to help you troubleshoot problems. If, for example, you're finding a particular task challenging to master, it might be that you need a better understanding of the subskills, and you need to break things down a little further. This will help you better understand where you're falling short.

Concreteness Fading

By now, you're probably getting a sense that deep, robust learning is all about creating solid connections:

- **Linking** all the bits of incoming data to one another in a web
- **Embedding** that web into your sensory world, into emotion, and into personal meaning and significance
- **Connecting** *that* web in turn to webs of pre-existing knowledge acquired earlier
- **Extrapolating** your entire body of skill and knowledge to other problems, situations, and contexts, thus expanding your reach

It's that final, extrapolating step that we'll consider in this chapter. The concept of **transfer** is about how we intelligently apply principles and learning from one area to another, unknown area. The only way we can do this, however, is to abstract those principles (i.e., make them theoretical and general enough that they can be used across a range of different situations). Transfer requires that we look beyond surface details and understand the organizing rules beneath them.

This takes some effort, because humans on the whole tend to work better with concrete information than abstract/general information. This preference, in fact, mirrors the way we learn things. First, we encounter a specific concrete problem, and then we encounter another, then another. Eventually we start to wonder if there is anything connecting these instances, and if we can take a shortcut by creating just *one* tool instead of reinventing the wheel each time, so to speak. The principle of scaffolding that we explored earlier on makes use of this phenomenon.

So, when we learn something, we typically start with the concrete . . . but that's not where we should stop if we hope to properly transfer our skills and knowledge elsewhere. We need to slowly and gradually move away from concrete/specific problems and solutions and move toward abstract mental representations of those problems and solutions.

This process of gradually moving from concrete to abstract is called concreteness fading. We can liken concreteness fading to that grey zone of proximal development that rests between what we do know and what we don't (can you see, in fact, that connecting Vygotsky's ZPD theory with the theory of concreteness fading is itself an example of what both these models are talking about?).

The image below is from education expert Dr. Carolina Kuepper-Tetzel and neatly encapsulates the *gradient* of change from initial learning to mastery. The process of replacing concrete components with abstract mental representations is smooth, not abrupt.

Initial Learning — *Mastery*

Provide concrete examples and work with concrete representations

Replace concrete components with abstract representations

Abstract representation

A study by Fyfe, McNeil, and Borja (2015) examined the effectiveness of three different styles of teaching. In the first study group, they tried to teach children how to do simple addition/equivalence math problems but in a concrete way—they used literal toys and objects to demonstrate the concepts directly and literally. For the second group they taught the same material but in a purely abstract way, i.e., with written number problems. In the third group they used concreteness fading, meaning they began with toys and objects, but then moved on to paper sums, thus gradually increasing the degree of abstraction.

Their results clearly favored the third group—these children were able to more quickly and effectively solve transfer problems compared to the other two groups. The poorest performance came from the concrete-only group. The study seems to confirm the old saying: "If you give a man a fish, he'll eat for a day. Teach him to fish and he'll eat for the rest of his life." The concrete-only group basically learned to do a single, discrete task, but the other two groups learned a *transferable skill* that could be applied to other tasks.

The following diagram from the educational website makemathmoments.com shows how concreteness fading may look in real life. You begin with a concrete representation of multiplication, and then you gently shift that representation toward more abstraction—the physical quantity is represented by numbers, and eventually the lines and multiplication symbol (x) come to stand for the operation in question. The transition is often best achieved through *visual* or *representational* means—i.e., some kind of diagram, symbol, or drawing that broaches the gap from **specific to general.**

Concreteness Fading

What's important here is that you find ways to blend both the concrete and abstract in your own learning and bootstrap your way from the particular to the universal. Indeed, concreteness fading itself can be considered a transferable skill since you can apply it to all your learning endeavors! As with everything the human brain does, we need to consistently consider context and what certain concepts actually mean in the real world.

Alphabets are an excellent organic example of this: Ancient alphabets began as pictorial representations of actual things in the environment they referenced. For example, the letter "A" evolved from a literal depiction of a bull's head, and the ancient Egyptian hieroglyph of an eye eventually became the letter "O."

Sometimes, without realizing that we're doing it, we actually approach the learning process *backward*—we start with an abstract idea, try to learn and master it, then practice applying it to specific examples. Another obvious problem is finding concrete examples but never moving on from them. It may feel as though you've mastered the underlying principle, but really, you've only mastered one specific instance of how the principle can be applied. That means that as soon as you're asked a question or given a challenge that even slightly deviates from the concrete example you learned, you're stumped.

If you asked a young pupil to figure out how many doughnuts were in a box, they may devise a way of finding the answer. If you employ concreteness fading, however, you can help them extract the rule behind their method and elicit from them the broader concept of multiplication, as shown below (again from the brilliant educational blog makemathmoments.com):

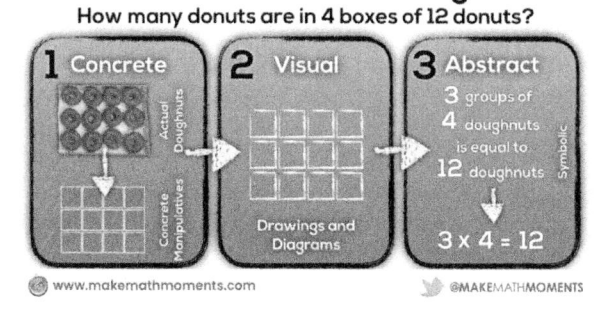

Concreteness Fading
How many donuts are in 4 boxes of 12 donuts?

1 Concrete — Actual Doughnuts / Concrete Manipulatives

2 Visual — Drawings and Diagrams

3 Abstract — 3 groups of 4 doughnuts is equal to 12 doughnuts

$$3 \times 4 = 12$$

www.makemathmoments.com @MAKEMATHMOMENTS

If you merely jump in and start to teach the pupils using the abstract version (i.e., 3 x 4 = 12), then from their point of view, it doesn't "mean" anything. If they understand how the rule of multiplication arose from the real, concrete world, however, they can understand how it can be used as a template to solve similar problems. That way, when you present them with a problem that's not about a handful of doughnuts but rather hundreds of thousands of dollars or atoms or people, they can instantly see that the *kind* of problem is the same as the one they've already mastered.

Kyle Pearce, the man behind makemathmoments.com, is a K-12 mathematics consultant and math learning expert, and he takes the above examples with doughnuts to greater and greater extremes, eventually showing how the power of concreteness fading can be extended to high school. Here the foundations laid in multiplication are extended to the cultivation of deeper algebraic reasoning that's required for thinking about linear and quadratic equations. This is all to say that although the doughnuts example will seem fairly simple, the principle itself can be applied to topics of all kinds and at all levels.

If you find yourself in the position of being your own teacher, then you are at an advantage since thinking carefully about concreteness fading in your own learning is itself a learning opportunity. How can you apply this concept to your own process?

Very simply, you start concrete and then gradually shift to more abstract. Let's break that down a little.

Step 1: Begin with concrete examples

Find tangible, real-world objects or situations to understand and master. For instance, if you're learning color theory, start by observing different objects around you and identifying their colors. You could also experiment with mixing paints or using color swatches to understand how colors interact and blend together.

Literally place different swatches next to one another and make observations, or play around with changing lighting or blending paints with white, grey, or brown to see what happens. You could also experiment in a similar way with colored lights and prisms, and compare these light experiments with your experiments using pigments.

Step 2: Start creating abstract representations of these examples

Gradually start introducing yourself to more abstract representations. This could involve learning about the concepts of color wheels, color schemes, and color harmonies through visual aids such as diagrams or illustrations. Start exploring how colors can evoke different emotions or convey different meanings in various contexts.

As you do so, however, remember that you are trying to *connect* the abstract to the concrete. So, for example, you may know in a literal way that red, yellow, and blue cannot be created by mixing other colors together, but that they themselves yield all sorts of other colors when combined.

You represent this characteristic of the colors red, blue, and yellow visually on a color wheel, and by placing this triad of colors in the center of the wheel. This diagrammatic depiction visually expresses the idea that the primary colors are fundamental, and that other colors derive from their combination:

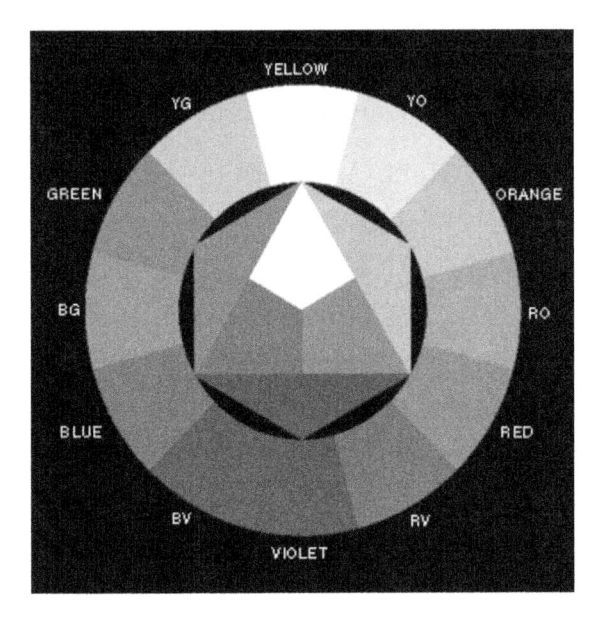

By examining the diagram above, you can probably see for yourself that it already suggests further shifts toward the abstract. If red and blue mixed together make violet, and so on, then you naturally wonder whether the rule can be iterated once more. What happens when you mix violet with another primary color? And if you then mix that color with a primary color or something else? *Why* does that happen—in other words, what are the rules that might govern these combinations? The diagram is what is prompting this kind of bridging thought process.

Step 3: Transition fully to abstract principles

Eventually, you are no longer dealing with paints and literal pigments, or even colored diagrams. The words "yellow" and "red" are the symbolic stand-ins for real-world phenomena. You go even further, however, and extend your learning to include abstract concepts such as hue, saturation, and brightness, and how they influence color perception and design choices.

You practice analyzing color compositions and creating color palettes without the need for direct reference to physical objects or visual aids. The words "a deeply toned grey-blue hue of medium saturation and low brightness" instantly conjures a specific image in your mind, as well as a host of attending theories.

Without needing to test it out in real life, you already know that a complementary shade to this color will be a similarly toned warm ochre. If you find an ochre shade that doesn't work somehow, you will instantly know to adjust the saturation or brightness levels. You know all this to be true in the same way that the math pupil knows that 3 x 4 is 12—that is, they know because of *internalized rules and theory*, not because they've taken the time to gather up three groups of four literal objects.

A few things to remember about concreteness fading:

The process is not meant to be terminal, but **cyclical**. In other words, once you've found abstract representations of your learning, cycle back and see how they can be applied once again to concrete problems. As in the above color example, you can apply your abstract principles to real and specific problems in the material world. Your knowledge of color theory can be applied to all sorts of design errors and problems. While others may end up wasting time with trial and error (i.e., they stay in the concrete realm), you can translate your abstract learning into solving problems well, even if you haven't encountered them before.

Something else to bear in mind is that concreteness fading is **iterative** and dynamic. Knowing how to make the next conceptual leap toward greater abstraction is sometimes the only way that you can solve a stubborn problem. If you're facing a plateau in learning, it may be a sign that you are being overly concrete and need to generalize. Take a look at a problem that's puzzling you and ask the following questions:

- What does this problem have in common with previous problems you've already solved?
- In what way is this problem completely different?
- What new skill or insight might you be lacking currently that would allow you to better grasp the problem?
- Can you find any useful metaphors or similes to help you better understand the concept?
- When you have been puzzled in the past, what kind of thinking allowed you to see beyond your problem?
- Is there someone who understands the thing you're struggling to understand? Can they teach you?
- What underlying principles have you already understood about this phenomenon?

- What happens when you deliberately try to solve this problem incorrectly? Why exactly doesn't it work, and what can that tell you about the things that *would* work?

If all else fails, it may simply be that you need to remain in the concrete stage for a little longer so that it's easier for you to begin identifying the abstract concepts that link all your specific examples together.

When we're learning something, it's easy to be impatient and want to quickly rush ahead to the end point where we imagine we have full mastery and total knowledge. But the truth is that learning and understanding only come to us as a *process*, bit by bit. If we rush past the first steps, we do not reach the later steps any faster, but merely miss out on all those things that would make our later understanding possible. Go slowly, don't be too hard on yourself, and when you encounter a wall, just become curious. "What is the invisible rule behind all this?"

Summary:

- Your outside is a reflection of our inside, and the degree of organization and logic in our external world mirrors the degree of organization in our internal world. Staying

organized improves the quality of your thought.
- The Zettelkasten method is an information management system and a method for more disciplined and effective thinking. Such a system enhances memory, reduces cognitive load, minimizes stress, helps you make connections and solve problems, and streamlines your study efforts.
- First read and annotate well according to your goal, then process the notes into a "zettel." Create links and references to connect to a web of learning, and continually review this web as part of your everyday workflow.
- You can have literature notes, reference notes, permanent notes, or fleeting notes according to their function in your broader organizational system. These notes can be categorized and organized in a meaningful way to express relationships and higher-order concepts, materially representing a "train of thought." Be patient, creative, and systematic, updating regularly. The dump, lump, and jump technique is a quick way to structure more creative processes.
- Every skill you possess is a composite of many other skills chunked together. Learning a skill is a multistep process. The

creation of a skill tree can help you better master a skill since it requires that you break down the skill into smaller hierarchical subskills according to your goals. This increases awareness, purposiveness, and directiveness in your learning journey. Construct a tree based on concepts, facts, and procedures, assess your current proficiency, and then get to work learning the skills in order, gradually fading from more concrete to more abstract as you go.
- Concreteness fading can help us transfer principles and learning from one area to another, as well as solve stubborn problems. Learning is best when it is iterative, cyclical, and dynamic.

Chapter 5: Mastering Mindset

In the previous chapter, we explored the complex interplay between concrete and abstract, as well as all the ways in which the external world becomes represented internally according to the way we organize ourselves and the material we're learning. By creating and following maps of our own learning process, we allow ourselves to take a step back and learn a little more about how we are learning. In this chapter, we will take a closer look at the psychology behind learning, and in particular how certain misconceptions and assumptions can hold us back from our full potential.

Thinking Modes: Focused or Diffuse?

In just the same way that abstract thinking is not better than concrete thinking, focused thinking is not necessarily superior to diffuse thinking.

What do we mean by focused and diffused?

Focused attention and thinking is fully invested in the single task in front of it. This is characterized by high levels of unbroken concentration channeled completely toward achieving its chosen outcome. It's like the intense, narrow beam of a laser.

Diffuse attention is the opposite and more spread out over a range of different stimuli, in a more free-form, relaxed, and responsive way, more like the softer but broader diffusion of a lamp—weaker but more expansive.

If you've spent any time at all in a conventional education setting in your life, you probably have absorbed the idea that focused attention is the ideal, and diffuse attention is the deviation that requires willpower and discipline to overcome. Many of us believe that if our attention wanders and we become distracted, the best response is to quickly pull it back to where it should be, through sheer self-control if possible, and eventually this will make us more "productive."

We can instead see both modes of thinking as valuable, however, and merely different from one another. While being able to completely screen out every piece of information unrelated to the task at hand is useful when we want to study a tricky concept or memorize something, what about all those times when paying attention to other pieces of information is actually necessary? To extend our metaphor, you certainly cannot cut steel with a gentle 60W lamp, but at the same time, a powerful laser is not the best way to bring some mood lighting into your living room!

The idea of diffuse versus focused thinking is said to have been popularized by professor of engineering Barbara Oakley. In her book *A Mind for Numbers: How to Excel at Math and Science (Even If You Flunked Algebra)*, she explains how people naturally switch between both modes.

Sometimes we require our brains to zoom in and do deep, highly focused work, and other times we need our conscious awareness to be looser, more open, and more receptive to the entire field of information around us—especially if we intend to discover something we don't know already, like a possible solution to our problem.

Now, diffuse thinking is not the same as being mindlessly distracted by social media or having a genuine inability to focus on the thing you'd like to focus on. Rather, diffuse thinking is that wide-angle lens on the world, the bigger-picture view. Letting your mind become unfocused and "wander" means it can freely explore connections, and this is the foundation of creativity. Hyperfocus necessarily means limitation, which is the opposite of what the creative mind does—expand.

Have you ever wondered why people have "eureka moments" when they're doing something mundane, or have "shower thoughts" at precisely those times in the day when they're not doing much of anything? Our greatest creativity and problem-solving moments often occur during loose, unprogrammed, and unstructured time—for example, on walks outside or during doodling or gazing mindlessly out the window . . . or even in dreams.

One misconception that's worth dropping, then, is the idea that diffuse thinking is a poor form of focused thinking, and that we can only ever learn or use our time well if we're ultra-focused. We need instead to expand our definition of discipline and productivity and appreciate that the brain has many modes, each of them valuable and appropriate for different kinds of tasks.

In fact, during the learning process, it may be that **switching consciously between the two modes brings the greatest benefit**. For example, we use focused thinking when we are taking in new information and seeking to nail down particular details, but then switch to diffuse thinking when we want to expand our awareness out into the context, the broader meaning, and the underlying principles. Very loosely, focused thinking suits concrete and specific tasks, and more diffuse thinking fits abstract and exploratory tasks.

We can oscillate between the two: We may learn a few concrete details and examples in a focused thirty-minute study session, then have a break, during which our unconscious mind passively absorbs and puts together what we've learned. We go in for another focused session, and end it with a more open-ended brainstorming session, where we play around using the concepts we've learned in a more creative way. Then we go in again once more for a focused session that analyses our output from this more open-ended work. In this way, both processes are spurring and feeding back into one another.

It's a little like an artist who zooms in and out of a large oil painting. First, he works on teeny-tiny details, getting up close to the picture and working with the more technical details, using his brush skills and so on. But periodically he needs to step back and look at the entire picture as a whole. He may even step away completely and "sleep on it" or go for a walk so that when he next turns up to the painting, he has a clearer idea of the overall impression, as well as how this translates down to the teeny-tiny details.

If the artist were to stay up close throughout the creation process, he may realize too late that he'd created a strange picture that was nevertheless technically correct in its details. The "Einstellung effect" is when we have too much concentrated focus on a single object—i.e., tunnel vision. Focused too much on what's directly in front of us, we lose the ability to think outside the box and cannot solve problems well because we are so firmly in the parameters that define that problem. We cannot see the forest for the trees.

That said, too much diffuse thinking that is not tempered by focused, detail-oriented work is going to fail for the opposite reason. The big picture may be there but the details are missing, and our understanding of specifics is limited.

The broader skill required here is not necessarily to become more disciplined or focused (although that is important) but rather to understand how and when to lean into your brain's different capacities depending on what's required. Deep work is a wonderful thing, but so is rest and daydreaming. Being organized and having scheduled time and clear goals is an excellent strategy, but so is making room for you to contemplate, unconsciously find connections, mull over things, and passively arrive at unexpected insights.

You can see this dynamic harmony play out in the way that some people read. They may read intently and with extreme focus for ten minutes or so, then let their eyes drift off the page as they digest what they've read. They repeat this process a few times in an hour, but they also mull over the book in the back of their mind as they go about the rest of their day.

In a 2014 *Psychology of Learning and Motivation* article (Schooler et al.), the authors claimed that "consciousness . . . ebbs like a breaking wave, outwardly expanding and then inwardly retreating. This perennial rhythm of the mind—extracting information from the external world, withdrawing to inner musings, and then returning to the outer realm—defines mental life."

We cannot stay ultra-focused for too long. It's uncomfortable, and we will rapidly lose effectiveness. It's even worse if we have bought into a host of core beliefs and assumptions about what it means to work hard or be intelligent. If we double down and label this natural mind-wandering as laziness or even procrastination (more on this later), then we are not only missing an opportunity to switch into useful diffuse thinking mode, but beating ourselves up in the process. Forcing yourself to stay focused when you're mentally exhausted can actually cement bad habits and encourage lazy mental shortcuts as your brain attempts to get away with doing less.

Particularly if we value creativity and novel insight, we need to **consciously make room for free-form mind wandering**. There is a long historical precedent for the value of this kind of open-ended passive "thinking":

- Richard Feynman found fresh insight into a tricky physics problem just by watching people spinning plates at his

university canteen one day while milling around doing nothing.
- Einstein is said to have come up with his relativity theory while having an argument with a friend (he later spent decades of focused thinking to refine this idea).
- German chemist August Kekule said that he discovered the structure of benzene (circular) after dreaming about a dragon eating its own tail.
- Salvador Dali made use of "micro naps" to tap his unconscious and generate his characteristic expression.
- Bach claims to have been struck with new ideas for symphonies while "on a break" walking in nature.

How can we make more deliberate use of both diffuse and focused thinking? One way is to be conscious of your energy levels and take fatigue as a sign that you need to rest and replenish. If you notice that after prolonged periods of work, your attention is wandering and you start to daydream, consider that this is not laziness but a prompt to step back, rest, and digest. Pushing on will only bring diminishing returns.

If you're worried that incorporating rest time will mean you lose out on focused time, you can put your mind at ease. Blending both forms of thinking, and moving with your own natural rhythms, often means you save time and are more effective in the long run.

Try to stick to short bursts of focused attention throughout the day. This way, you make more efficient use of your time and also free up room for diffuse thinking time. For example, fifteen minutes of ultra-focused time, followed by forty-five minutes of diffuse wandering and relaxation, may ultimately generate more benefits than scheduling fifty minutes of grueling work, losing interest after ten minutes, then wasting the remaining time only half engaged but full of guilt and with almost nothing left over for contemplation or rest. Both strategies will use an hour of time, but that same hour will yield very different results.

Tips for Being a More Rounded Thinker

Start with focused thinking: Begin by immersing yourself in focused thinking to understand the fundamental concepts of a topic without distractions. You can think of this as your opportunity to drill down to concrete examples, facts, and data. Allocate dedicated time and space for focused learning where you can delve deeply into the subject matter, absorbing key details and building a solid foundation of knowledge.

For example, you may begin a practice session on the violin by starting with a warmup exercise and scales, going over them again and again and practicing the details of your technical skills.

Transition to diffuse thinking: After you've done an intense sprint of focused thinking, it's time to relax and pull back a little. Do this gradually and give yourself some time to absorb and internalize the new information and start making connections with what you already know how to do.

In the violin example, you may take a quick five-minute snack break or quickly review previous scales (you're scaffolding in the process) and recap yesterday's practice points. Then you can allow your mind to wander and explore various associations and insights related to the topic. In the case of playing the violin, you can spontaneously let your fingers play around with the scale and see what emerges. What melodies spring to mind? What are you reminded of? What interesting associations have you noticed?

Refine connections in focused mode: After spending some time resting and exploring in diffuse thinking mode, return to a more focused state of mind and review your insights. What does your more focused, deliberate brain think of the associations you came up with? Now's the time to logically appraise and analyze them and see how they can be worked into your more deliberate practice moving forward.

Maybe you notice that you'd like to move on to practicing a certain piece that fits more naturally with the scale you practiced, or maybe you make a note about an alluring tune you came up with that you'd like to elaborate on at a later date. Many jazz musicians work this way: They spend time in an almost transcendental state of free-forming improvisation, but almost always return to particularly interesting parts that emerged so they can select, reinforce, and integrate them into future creations.

Finally, repeat the process: Learning is iterative; every time the cycle turns, it refines itself, amplifying the good and chiseling away at the bad until the goal is achieved.

The Procrastination Equation

As we near the end of our book, it's time to consider the phenomenon of procrastination—something that most of us unfortunately have dealt with at some point in our lives. In reading the previous section, you might have wondered, "What's the difference between taking a well-earned break and plain old procrastinating?" Or, to expand on this, "How do I tell the difference between a genuine reason to not work and a mere excuse?"

These are good questions. If you've struggled with putting off tasks in the past, you've probably already sensed that procrastination is more of an umbrella term for many different habits, behaviors, and attitudes. Piers Steel is a productivity expert and was interested in this very question, eventually proposing what he called the "procrastination equation." He wanted to really understand how it was that people could sincerely want to work on a task yet found themselves repeatedly avoiding it.

Before we look at Steel's equation, let's be real about a few things: Sometimes the reason we don't take the action we said we'd take is completely legitimate. Perhaps there aren't enough resources (time, energy), or your goals have shifted. Perhaps the task is just objectively unpleasant (boring chores, stressful but necessary errands) and your avoidance is only human and nothing out of the ordinary. Perhaps on second thought you really *don't* want to do this task as much as you thought you did, and you need a more serious reappraisal of your goals and intentions.

But the following equation is for those moments of genuine procrastination—i.e., where we can comfortably exclude other causes of avoidance and distraction. How will you know if your "reason" is just an excuse? Well, a good hint is how you feel—if most of us are honest, we know precisely when we are being lazy, and procrastination usually comes along with mild feelings of anxiety, guilt, and shame that alert us to the fact that we are falling short of our standards and values.

The procrastination equation is as follows:

Motivation = (Expectancy x Value) / (Impulsiveness x Delay)

To put that into words: Our total motivation to work on a task is composed of how much we expect to succeed at it (expectancy) multiplied by how much value we place on the task (value) divided by the product of two further factors—our impulsiveness and the time we have left before we reach that goal's deadline.

What the equation suggests is that **we can improve motivation and decrease procrastination by working at increasing expectancy and value, and decreasing impulsivity and delay**. The equation also tells us that procrastination is a dish that can be made of different ingredients in different proportions. If you've ever tried to apply some procrastination tips and tricks and found them useless, this may be why. Not all procrastination is created equal, and what works for one kind may not work for another. The equation can help you understand exactly where your procrastination is coming from so that you can take steps that fit you and your situation.

The first thing, then, is to build awareness of where you are right now and what you're actually doing. Simply saying, "I'm procrastinating," is not a detailed enough explanation. Gain more insight by working through each of the four variables in the equation.

Expectancy: Do You Actually Believe You Can Succeed?

This variable is huge but usually overlooked. Sometimes, we put off doing a task because deep down, we don't actually think we have any chance of succeeding at it. Imagine that someone asked you to flip a coin, and if it came up heads, you'd win a prize. You'd be motivated to try it, in all likelihood. Imagine they then told you that no matter what, the coin would always come up tails, and you had no chance of winning anything. What happens to your motivation to flip that coin?

We may hold unconscious beliefs about our abilities (low) or the difficulty of the task (high) that lead to us leap to foregone conclusions that we will fail. Carrying doubt about your chances of success will drain away any motivation, courage, or hope you have for the task. In essence, your procrastination is a little like giving up, and your disengagement is actually a rational choice if you will indeed only fail at the task.

Of course, the trouble is that our appraisals of our own abilities or the difficulty of the task are often distorted, and so our expectancy about a situation may be entirely down to our own perception, and not the realities of the situation. Do you secretly believe that your efforts, no matter how noble, won't really pay off in the end? Do you quietly think, "I'm just going through the motions. None of this is going to make a difference anyway"?

If so, you need to get honest and clear about how you are spending your time and resources. In particular, *you need to understand whether your appraisal of the futility of the situation is actually accurate or not.* Occasionally, you really are faced with a task that is beyond you, and the best way forward is not to attempt it. More likely, though, you just lack confidence.

To overcome this, try to source inspirational talks, books, articles, or podcasts that get you feeling inspired and encouraged. Break your task into smaller chunks and make a point of congratulating and praising yourself for each milestone. Really *practice* believing that you are capable and can do it.

Make a list of all the positive feedback you've received from people, or actively ask for more (you may be surprised how forthcoming it is!). Another tip is to look back and consider all the things you've already accomplished. Consider how in the past you may have felt incompetent and afraid, but triumphed in the end. What did you do in the past to succeed? Can you imagine yourself carrying that forward to your current situation?

Value: Can You Find Value in the Things You Don't Like?

We are more motivated to do the things we feel are valuable. Everyone can find motivation to attend their own wedding or drive to the pharmacy to collect medication that will save their lives. Not all tasks are going to *feel* this valuable in the moment, however. In fact, **many of the things we commit to doing are going to be tasks we hate**. Going to the gym on a dark winter morning, filing taxes, going to bed even though we'd rather binge watch a TV series . . .

Again, however, it comes down to perception. If you often find yourself saying something to the effect of, "I want to, but I don't want to . . ." then you may need to change how you think about value. One of the biggest misconceptions in life is that we can only act toward a chosen goal if we *feel* like it in the moment. Unless we are motivated and find something enjoyable, we think, then we don't have to act, or shouldn't have to. Really, the reverse is true. We can set a goal for ourselves that we cherish more than anything in life, and which aligns perfectly with our values and who we want to be . . . and it can still feel boring, scary, or uninspiring to take action toward that goal.

If you find it easy to dream big but difficult to act small, then *try to find ways to better connect your actions in the present to your larger, overarching goals*. Going to the gym on a dark winter morning may not feel good, but what does feel good is knowing that going anyway makes you stronger and builds your integrity. You don't derive pleasure from dragging yourself out of bed and heading out in the cold, but you do feel pleasure in the knowledge that you are cultivating discipline and that your efforts will pay off in the future.

If you focus exclusively on all the parts of early-morning workouts that you hate, you can easily convince yourself that this is something life is forcing you to do and that you really hate it. So, you don't go. But if you can draw your attention to how this gym behavior connects to your bigger values and goals, you can encourage yourself to see the good in it—and you're more likely to do it.

Importantly, shifting your perspective is not about denying how difficult/unpleasant/inconvenient a task is. Rather, it's about reframing what that difficulty *means*, and choosing to choose it! It also doesn't hurt to find ways to make it more immediately enjoyable—can you listen to an interesting audiobook on your way to the gym? What about a nice healthy treat as a reward when you get home?

Impulsiveness: What Can You Do to Subdue the Demon?

You may have high expectancy, and you may really value what you're doing, but if you succumb to impulsivity, you can still derail yourself and fall short of your potential. This variable in the equation is simple but difficult to shift because it stems from a very stubborn feature of human nature. If we're engaged in something difficult and demanding, it's all too easy to have our attention taken by some other task that is relatively more pleasant. Call it "**shiny object syndrome**." In an attempt to optimize, we switch to something that promises to deliver good feelings and rewards for less effort. In other words, instant gratification always looks like a better deal when your alternative feels like a boring slog.

The first thing to do here is to acknowledge that the human default is a preference for *exploration* (things we want to do) over *exploitation* (things we have to do). We might initially choose a goal because it's novel and we want to do it, but over time we lose interest and momentum, and it becomes a thing we have to do . . . and so we scan around, looking for something new to give us that initial buzz again. The reward for our current task may be greater, but it'll only be available at some distant point in the future. The reward for attending to some immediate distraction may be pretty small, but it's "low hanging fruit" that's right there for the taking.

To master the impulsivity demon, you need to be prepared. Recognize that this innate preference is working in you, and take proactive steps to avoid or mitigate it. By actively shaping your environment and making choices for yourself that *pre-empt* all those little temptations and distractions, you give yourself a better chance of resisting them. Keep known temptations well out of sight—for example, put your phone in the next room and close the door.

Clear your desk, disconnect from the internet, hang a Do Not Disturb sign on your door, and don't give yourself any opportunity to wander. If something pops up, don't waste too much energy arguing with the impulse. Just make a note somewhere and continue working. Tell yourself, "Thanks, brain, I'll look at that later. But now, I'm working." Repeat as necessary.

Delay: Do You Need to Be More Realistic About Time?

Deadlines that are set far in the future tend to decrease your motivation—the greater the value for "delay" in the equation, the lower your motivation will be. The trouble is that the best and most valuable goals tend to be rather large, and so they necessarily only come to fruition far into the future, sometimes so far that we only have a vague sense of when we'll achieve them.

To decrease this value in the equation, the idea is not to bring the deadline artificially close (that will only stress you out!) but rather to work with your perception of where the point of accomplishment is. Here, smaller goals that you pause to acknowledge and celebrate are going to create the illusion that there isn't much of a delay between your effort and the outcome of that effort.

Make sure your deadlines are realistic (it's a good habit to add about twenty percent more time than you guess you'll need), but think about creating smaller deadlines in the interim. You may feel more of a sense of reward and progress from a series of five smaller projects than a single reward that's five times as large. Create a routine and stick to it, keeping close track of how you're advancing every day, every hour. You want to cultivate the sense that every minute you spend on your task brings you a tiny bit closer to the goal.

A Quick Procrastination Troubleshooting Process

The procrastination equation is great for figuring out your habits and mindset more generally, but it won't be much help in the heat of the moment. The best insight is to be gained from paying attention to your own procrastination process as it unfolds.

Step 1: Actually notice that you are procrastinating

Pause and observe. Give the thing a name. Be honest with yourself! Be very clear about what it was you set out to do, and what you did instead. At what point did your motivation drop? What kind of task and goal are you working with, and do you have the necessary tools and information to do it properly? What was your strategy for doing the task?

Step 2: Ask yourself WHY

Without shame or judgment, get curious about exactly where the problem is right now in the moment. You can then consider which of the four variables in the equation are lacking, but don't necessarily take your own word for it. Your first few answers to the WHY question may be excuses that conceal the deeper reasons, so you may need to keep digging for the truth. You want to identify whether the problem is impulsiveness, a value misperception, a delay, etc.

Step 3: Do something!

Naturally, you want to take action to address the problem you've identified. Take action, even if it's small. If the issue is impulsiveness, do something right now to modify your environment so you're relying less on raw willpower. If it's a value problem, pause for a second to remind yourself of why you're doing any of it, or take a few minutes to fully visualize your goal and find the good in the boring task in front of you.

If you're having difficulty identifying the issue, take a step back, perhaps chatting the problem over with someone else or writing things out to slow your thought process. It may be that all four equation factors are at play.

Step 4: Play around with alternatives

Let's be honest: Life is often messy, and your situation may genuinely not fit into the equation. If you're really not finding a way forward, there may be a more subtle way around your current mental block.

If you're not on a very tight deadline, could you switch to another task for the time being and return to this one a little later (remembering the value of diffuse thinking)? Perhaps you're not demotivated so much as hungry, cold, or upset about something else? It may be that a quick power nap or vigorous walk is all you need to bring in some fresh new energy.

Whatever you do, there's little value in beating yourself up about being lazy, undisciplined, or unproductive. It's far more worth your time (and less stressful) to simply get curious about what is happening and why, and commit to taking small action in the right direction.

Play Matters!

So far, we've considered the ideas of all kinds of experts and authorities, but perhaps we should be most curious about those true experts of learning: children. Though we may take their efforts for granted, nobody learns anything faster than a young child. The way they learn, however, is not to use mind maps, mnemonics, or gimmicky productivity hacks. Rather, their method is *play*.

In the amusingly titled *Einstein Never Used Flashcards: How Our Children Really Learn—and Why They Need to Play More and Memorize Less*, authors Roberta Michnick Golinkoff and Kathy Hirsh-Pasek explore all the ways that young children really learn, and how conventional education and parenting gets it all wrong. Our societal expectations about what counts as "educational" carry over to our adult lives, and we seem to hold on to the belief that work and play are two very, very different things.

In the book, the authors address several myths about children and how they learn, but they apply just as much to adults:

- First, that you don't necessarily need complicated gadgets and tricks; what you

really need is real-world examples that mean something to you.
- Learning needs to be embedded in the real world and relational. Make things experiential. Connect.
- Create an environment around you that supports your learning. Instead of having discrete learning chunks here and there, make learning a permanent and pervasive part of everyday life.
- Explore, enjoy your environment, play, be curious, seek stimulation, and interact with others—learning is meant to be *used* in the real world.
- IQ is not the be-all and end-all. Pay attention to your social skills, your emotional regulation, and your ability to reflect and be self-aware.
- Finally, no matter what, keep asking questions!

You may think that play and exploration is fine for young kids, but that adults need to get on with the hard work of life. In reality, **we can all benefit from a more open-ended, playful, and natural approach to learning no matter our age or our chosen field of learning**. Play is not something reserved for children, but is an ingrained part of our evolutionary history and a big reason for our species' survival. Think of play as *engagement with the environment* and you'll see that it can take on many forms.

Healthy humans naturally expand and explore their environments. It's the basis of our problem-solving, exploration, and creativity. We can even consider play a mindset or mode of thinking, rather than a set of actions. All we need to embrace its power is to drop any preconceptions of it being irrelevant or indulgent.

When you play, you engage more deeply. Your attention is sustained for a longer period. You remember more. You're more focused on working through problems and more resilient as the challenge dials up. You're more creative, and you come up with more innovative and original solutions.

Author and play expert Dr. Stuart Brown explains in his book *Play: How It Shapes the Brain, Opens the Imagination, and Invigorates the Soul* that play is not just preconscious or preverbal, but deeply primal. We "are designed to find fulfilment and creative growth through play" he claims, and this biological urge is just as important as the drive for eating or sleeping. We all need to play, and we all know how to play—it's just a question of *remembering how*.

Find More Joy, More Curiosity, More Exploration . . .

Here we arrive at a conundrum—trying to be serious about play is a little like trying to be organized about spontaneity. The idea is not to give yourself a rigid set of tasks to tick off a list. Rather, play is about a mental orientation. It's less about "How do I . . .?" and more about "What's possible . . .? What if . . .? This looks interesting. What's this . . .?"

In that spirit, here are some tips and guidelines to point you in the right direction. Bear in mind that you were once a play expert in the past!

Reconnect to Storytelling

There's a reason that kids love stories so much. Narratives are part of the DNA of human experience. We embed meaning, context, and consequence into the stories we tell. It's how we learn about cause and effect, how we identify people off of whom to model ourselves, how we orient to worldviews and mental models, how we learn to solve problems and identify patterns, and of course, how we develop an aesthetic and lyrical sense of the world.

Stories make the world mean something. If you're learning about history, try to dig deep and find the narratives that would make that content come to life. Even if your chosen topic of learning is fairly abstract, find ways to immerse yourself and bring a human element to everything you encounter. You'll instantly make things more memorable in the process.

Reconnect to Humor

Somewhere along the line we learn that enjoyment, silliness, fun, and absurdity are in opposition to good work and progress. Nothing could be further from the truth! Humor is one of the brain's many legitimate modes of processing and can often unlock new insight, unrecognized solutions, or novel perspectives on what would otherwise seem boring and obvious.

Humor *is* creativity. If you want to find more flexibility in your studies and in the way you think in general, humor is a powerful but underappreciated faculty. Make things up. Put strange combinations together just because they amuse you. Look at things back to front and enjoy being a little off-the-wall now and then. Often, we are making active efforts not to see how bizarre and funny life really is. All you have to do is put yourself in the shoes of that curious child who really is seeing life for the first time. Isn't the world so marvelously *odd* sometimes?

Reconnect to Your Imagination

It might not always look like it, but kids are masters of simulation and abstract symbolic representation—only they call it "make-believe." You can enhance your own perspective-taking abilities by engaging in a little role play, which will also give you a potentially useful alternative view on a situation. It's silly when a children's TV show character says something like, "If I were a magical frog, where would I most likely be hiding?" But this kind of "game" cultivates empathy and a deeper and richer understanding of all the elements in a problem or situation.

Your imagination gives you access to metaphors, imagery, and analogies that allow you to grasp new concepts more easily, not to mention communicate those concepts to others. Making things tangible is a way that children build a bridge from what they know to what they don't yet know, and you can do the same.

Reconnect to Your Rebelliousness

Sometimes children's greatest genius is to be a little wild and nonconforming to the adult world. Their gift is to see the world as it really is, rather than what they've been taught it is. You can tap into this by giving yourself permission to explore controversial or alternative ideas and viewpoints that a more "grown-up" version of you would find a waste of time.

Switch up context, ask awkward questions, push limits, or dare to look at things in a completely different way. Not only will this help you shift perspective, but it may also energize and inspire you—nothing brings more enthusiasm into a stale old project quicker than an unexpected, slightly dangerous opinion!

Reconnect to Your Emotions

Children bring their entire selves to the process of exploration and engagement. They are not cold, detached, and aloof scientists far removed from the world. They get their hands dirty, so to speak, and they immerse fully in the work of play—body, mind, and soul.

If you're feeling stagnant and uninspired, it may be that you've allowed your emotions to become dampened. Can you remind yourself of why you started your learning journey in the first place? Can you remember the passion, burning curiosity, or sense of wonder that you first had when you encountered the unknown? By reconnecting to your emotional engagement with your material, you instantly make it more human, more meaningful, and more personal. And this in turn can bring enormous amounts of motivation and drive to what may have become a dry academic exercise over time.

Learning Is the Work of a Lifetime

Throughout this book, we've considered many different theories and approaches and tried to apply them to a variety of specific examples. Learning to learn will obviously help you pass an exam or master a new set of skills, but hopefully over time it offers something greater than that. Learning is not just a neat ability that we pull out of the bag now and then whenever we need it. Rather, it's a way of life, an attitude, and a total philosophy that touches everything we do.

In the preceding chapters, we learned about the value not just of working with the underlying structure and logic of learning, but also with the more abstract, psychological, and relational aspects of the learning process. Learning is a practical daily habit but also a set of beliefs and emotions; it's the capacity to work hard and stay focused and organized, but it's also the willingness to remain forever open and curious, to try something new, and to keep reflexively looking back at the way we're using our brains. It's wonderful to know that no matter our chosen field of study, the difficulty of the task, or our current skill level, we always have access to this process of improvement—and it's a process that we will never exhaust.

Summary:

- There are two modes of thinking: focused attention (concentrated, narrow, and singular) and diffuse attention (free-form, open, and exploratory). Neither is superior to the other, but both can be useful, especially when combined. Focused attention is best for analysis, deep work, and memorizing, while diffuse attention is

best for contemplation, creativity, and processing.
- Learn to consciously switch between focused and diffuse, and make room for free-form mind wandering and unstructured time in your schedule. Procrastination is an umbrella term for many different habits, behaviors, and attitudes. The procrastination equation can help us understand the factors behind our own procrastination so we can take targeted action to fix the problem. Being a problem of motivation, the equation goes like this: **Motivation = (Expectancy x Value) / (Impulsiveness x Delay)**.
- We can improve motivation and decrease procrastination by increasing expectancy and value and decreasing impulsivity and delay—or a combination of these. Determine expectancy by asking if you sincerely believe you can succeed. Build expectancy by increasing self-esteem and reward. Increase value by finding the good in the tasks you don't want to do and reframing your attitude. Reduce impulsiveness by changing your environment so it tempts you less. Decrease delay by breaking tasks down, tracking progress, and acknowledging your milestones.

- Reappraise unconscious beliefs about your abilities, the difficulty of the task, or how to respond to boredom or discomfort. Connect your action in the present to your larger, overarching goals, and reconnect to the bigger meaning. Pre-empt temptations and distractions and proactively shape your environment to mitigate them. Be realistic with time management.
- Play is an essential and valuable part of the learning process. To bring more play into your life, find ways to incorporate stories, humor, emotion, imagination, wonder, embodiment, enjoyment, exploration, curiosity, silliness, or even a little rebelliousness into your learning process.

Printed in Great Britain
by Amazon